MznLnx

Missing Links Exam Preps

Exam Prep for

Finite Mathematics For Business, Economics, Life Sciences, And Social Sciences

Barnett, Ziegler, Byleen, 10th Edition

The MznLnx Exam Prep is your link from the texbook and lecture to your exams.
The MznLnx Exam Preps are unauthorized and comprehensive reviews of your textbooks.

All material provided by MznLnx and Rico Publications (c) 2010
Textbook publishers and textbook authors do not particpate in or contribute to these reviews.

MznLnx

Rico Publications

Exam Prep for Finite Mathematics For Business, Economics, Life Sciences, And Social Sciences
10th Edition
Barnett, Ziegler, Byleen

Publisher: Raymond Houge	*Product Manager:* Dave Mason
Assistant Editor: Michael Rouger	*Editorial Assitant:* Rachel Guzmanji
Text and Cover Designer: Lisa Buckner	*Pedagogy:* Debra Long
Marketing Manager: Sara Swagger	*Cover Image:* Jim Reed/Getty Images
Project Manager, Editorial Production: Jerry Emerson	*Text and Cover Printer:* City Printing, Inc.
Art Director: Vernon Lowerui	*Compositor:* Media Mix, Inc.

(c) 2010 Rico Publications

ALL RIGHTS RESERVED. No part of this work covered by the copyright may be reproduced or used in any form or by an means--graphic, electronic, or mechanical, including photocopying, recording, taping, Web distribution, information storage, and retrieval systems, or in any other manner--without the written permission of the publisher.

For more information about our products, contact us at:

Dave.Mason@RicoPublications.com

For permission to use material from this text or product, submit a request online to:

Dave.Mason@RicoPublications.com

Printed in the United States
ISBN:

Contents

CHAPTER 1
A Beginning Library of Elementary Functions — 1

CHAPTER 2
Additional Elementary Functions — 18

CHAPTER 3
Mathematics of Finance — 31

CHAPTER 4
Systems of Linear Equations; Matrices — 36

CHAPTER 5
Linear Inequalities and Linear Programming — 49

CHAPTER 6
Logic, Sets, and Counting — 61

CHAPTER 7
Probability — 72

CHAPTER 8
Data Description and Probability Distributions — 86

CHAPTER 9
Games and Decisions — 104

CHAPTER 10
Markov Chains — 107

CHAPTER 11
Basic Algebra Review — 112

ANSWER KEY — 136

TO THE STUDENT

COMPREHENSIVE

The *MznLnx* Exam Prep series is designed to help you pass your exams. Editors at MznLnx review your textbooks and then prepare these practice exams to help you master the textbook material. Unlike study guides, workbooks, and practice tests provided by the texbook publisher and textbook authors, *MznLnx* gives you **all** of the material in each chapter in exam form, not just samples, so you can be sure to nail your exam.

MECHANICAL

The MznLnx Exam Prep series creates exams that will help you learn the subject matter as well as test you on your understanding. Each question is designed to help you master the concept. Just working through the exams, you gain an understanding of the subject--its a simple mechanical process that produces success.

INTEGRATED STUDY GUIDE AND REVIEW

MznLnx is not just a set of exams designed to test you, its also a comprehensive review of the subject content. Each exam question is also a review of the concept, making sure that you will get the answer correct without having to go to other sources of material. You learn as you go! Its the easiest way to pass an exam.

HUMOR

Studying can be tedious and dry. MznLnx's instructional design includes moderate humor within the exam questions on occassion, to break the tedium and revitalize the brain

Chapter 1. A Beginning Library of Elementary Functions 1

1. The x-axis is the horizontal axis of a two- dimensional plot in the _____, that is typically pointed to the right. Also known as a right-handed coordinate system.
   a. 120-cell
   b. 1-center problem
   c. 2-3 heap
   d. Cartesian coordinate system

2. In quantum field theory and statistical mechanics in the thermodynamic limit, a system with a global symmetry can have more than one phase. For parameters where the symmetry is spontaneously broken, the system is said to be _____. When the global symmetry is unbroken the system is disordered.
   a. Ordered
   b. Ursell function
   c. Einstein relation
   d. Isoenthalpic-isobaric ensemble

3. In mathematics, an _____ is a collection of objects having two coordinates (or entries or projections), such that one can always uniquely determine the object, which is the first coordinate (or first entry or left projection) of the pair as well as the second coordinate (or second entry or right projection.) If the first coordinate is a and the second is b, the usual notation for an _____ is (a, b.) The pair is 'ordered' in that (a, b) differs from (b, a) unless a = b.
   a. A chemical equation
   b. Ordered pair
   c. A posteriori
   d. A Mathematical Theory of Communication

4. In mathematics, the _____ of a Euclidean space is a special point, usually denoted by the letter O, used as a fixed point of reference for the geometry of the surrounding space. In a Cartesian coordinate system, the _____ is the point where the axes of the system intersect. In Euclidean geometry, the _____ may be chosen freely as any convenient point of reference.
   a. Autonomous system
   b. Origin
   c. Interval
   d. OMAC

5. A _____ consists of one quarter of the coordinate plane.

a. Quadrant
b. 1-center problem
c. 2-3 heap
d. 120-cell

6. In mathematics, the Cartesian coordinate system is used to determine each point uniquely in a plane through two numbers, usually called the x-coordinate or _____ and the y-coordinate or ordinate of the point. To define the coordinates, two perpendicular directed lines, are specified, as well as the unit length, which is marked off on the two axes. Cartesian coordinate systems are also used in space and in higher dimensions.
   a. Elliptic cylindrical coordinates
   b. Oblate spheroidal coordinates
   c. Astronomical coordinate systems
   d. Abscissa

7. _____ is the study of geometry using the principles of algebra. That the algebra of the real numbers can be employed to yield results about the linear continuum of geometry relies on the Cantor-Dedekind axiom. Usually the Cartesian coordinate system is applied to manipulate equations for planes, straight lines, and squares, often in two and sometimes in three dimensions of measurement.
   a. Angular eccentricity
   b. Axis-aligned object
   c. Ambient space
   d. Analytic geometry

8. _____ is a part of mathematics concerned with questions of size, shape, and relative position of figures and with properties of space. _____ is one of the oldest sciences. Initially a body of practical knowledge concerning lengths, areas, and volumes, in the third century BC _____ was put into an axiomatic form by Euclid, whose treatment--Euclidean _____--set a standard for many centuries to follow.
   a. 120-cell
   b. 1-center problem
   c. Geometry
   d. 2-3 heap

9. In mathematics, a _____ is a statement that can be proved on the basis of explicitly stated or previously agreed assumptions.

a. Disjunction introduction
b. Logical value
c. Boolean function
d. Theorem

10. A _____ is an algebraic equation in which each term is either a constant or the product of a constant and a single variable. _____s can have one, two, three or more variables.

_____s occur with great regularity in applied mathematics.

a. Quadratic equation
b. Quartic equation
c. Linear equation
d. Difference of two squares

11. _____ generally conveys two primary meanings. The first is an imprecise sense of harmonious or aesthetically-pleasing proportionality and balance; such that it reflects beauty or perfection. The second meaning is a precise and well-defined concept of balance or 'patterned self-similarity' that can be demonstrated or proved according to the rules of a formal system: by geometry, through physics or otherwise.
a. Symmetry breaking
b. Tessellation
c. Molecular symmetry
d. Symmetry

12. In mathematics, especially in the area of abstract algebra known as ring theory, a _____ is a ring with $0 \neq 1$ such that ab = 0 implies that either a = 0 or b = 0. That is, it is a nontrivial ring without left or right zero divisors. A commutative _____ is called an integral _____.
a. Domain
b. Simple ring
c. Modular representation theory
d. Left primitive ring

13. The mathematical concept of a _____ expresses the intuitive idea of deterministic dependence between two quantities, one of which is viewed as primary and the other as secondary. A _____ then is a way to associate a unique output for each input of a specified type, for example, a real number or an element of a given set.

a. Function
b. Coherent
c. Going up
d. Grill

14. In descriptive statistics, the _____ is the length of the smallest interval which contains all the data. It is calculated by subtracting the smallest observations from the greatest and provides an indication of statistical dispersion.

It is measured in the same units as the data.

a. Range
b. Kernel
c. Class
d. Bandwidth

15. In mathematics, the _____ of a real number is its numerical value without regard to its sign. So, for example, 3 is the _____ of both 3 and −3.

The _____ of a number a is denoted by $|a|$.

Generalizations of the _____ for real numbers occur in a wide variety of mathematical settings.

a. A Mathematical Theory of Communication
b. Absolute value
c. Area hyperbolic functions
d. A chemical equation

16. _____ and independent variables refer to values that change in relationship to each other. The _____ are those that are observed to change in response to the independent variables. The independent variables are those that are deliberately manipulated to invoke a change in the _____.

a. Dependent variables
b. Yates analysis
c. Steiner system
d. Round robin test

17. Dependent variables and _____ refer to values that change in relationship to each other. The dependent variables are those that are observed to change in response to the _____. The _____ are those that are deliberately manipulated to invoke a change in the dependent variables.

a. Operational confound
b. Experimental design diagram
c. One-factor-at-a-time method
d. Independent variables

18. In mathematics, _____ and undefined are used to explain whether or not expressions have meaningful, sensible, and unambiguous values. Not all branches of mathematics come to the same conclusion.

The following expressions are undefined in all contexts, but remarks in the analysis section may apply.

a. Plugging in
b. LHS
c. Defined
d. Toy model

19. In mathematics, a _____ is the end result of a division problem. It can also be expressed as the number of times the divisor divides into the dividend.
a. Limiting
b. Marginal cost
c. Notation
d. Quotient

20. In economics, business, retail, and accounting, a _____ is the value of money that has been used up to produce something, and hence is not available for use anymore. In business, the _____ may be one of acquisition, in which case the amount of money expended to acquire it is counted as _____. In this case, money is the input that is gone in order to acquire the thing.
a. Cost
b. 120-cell
c. 2-3 heap
d. 1-center problem

21. In economics, the cross elasticity of demand and _____ measures the responsiveness of the quantity demanded of a good to a change in the price of another good.

It is measured as the percentage change in quantity demanded for the first good that occurs in response to a percentage change in price of the second good. For example, if, in response to a 10% increase in the price of fuel, the quantity of new cars that are fuel inefficient demanded decreased by 20%, the cross elasticity of demand would be -20%/10% = -2.

Chapter 1. A Beginning Library of Elementary Functions

a. Cross price elasticity of demand
b. Supply and demand
c. 1-center problem
d. Marginal rate of substitution

22. _____ consists of 'social relations involving authority or power' and refers to the regulation of a political unit, and to the methods and tactics used to formulate and apply policy.

Political science (also political studies) is the study of political behavior, and examines the acquisition and application of power. Related areas of study include political philosophy, which seeks a rationale for _____ and an ethic of public behavior, and public administration, which examines the practices of governance.

a. 2-3 heap
b. 120-cell
c. Politics
d. 1-center problem

23. A _____ of a number is a number a such that $a^3 = x$.
a. Square root
b. Cube root
c. Golden function
d. Hyperbolic functions

24. In mathematics, the term _____ has several different important meanings:

- An _____ is an equality that remains true regardless of the values of any variables that appear within it, to distinguish it from an equality which is true under more particular conditions. For this, the 'triple bar' symbol ≡ is sometimes used.
- In algebra, an _____ or _____ element of a set S with a binary operation Â· is an element e that, when combined with any element x of S, produces that same x. That is, eÂ·x = xÂ·e = x for all x in S.
    - The _____ function from a set S to itself, often denoted id or id_S, s the function such that i = x for all x in S. This function serves as the _____ element in the set of all functions from S to itself with respect to function composition.
    - In linear algebra, the _____ matrix of size n is the n-by-n square matrix with ones on the main diagonal and zeros elsewhere. This matrix serves as the _____ with respect to matrix multiplication.

A common example of the first meaning is the trigonometric _____

$$\sin^2 \theta + \cos^2 \theta = 1$$

which is true for all real values of θ, as opposed to

$$\cos \theta = 1,$$

which is true only for some values of θ, not all. For example, the latter equation is true when $\theta = 0$, false when $\theta = 2$

The concepts of 'additive _____' and 'multiplicative _____' are central to the Peano axioms. The number 0 is the 'additive _____' for integers, real numbers, and complex numbers. For the real numbers, for all $a \in \mathbb{R}$,

$$0 + a = a,$$

$$a + 0 = a, \text{ and}$$

$$0 + 0 = 0.$$

Similarly, The number 1 is the 'multiplicative _____' for integers, real numbers, and complex numbers.

a. ARIA
b. Intersection
c. Action
d. Identity

25. An _____ is a function that does not have any effect: it always returns the same value that was used as its argument.
a. Identity function
b. Inverse function
c. Algebra
d. Angle bisector

26. In mathematics, a _____ is a square root of a function with respect to the operation of function composition. In other words, the functional square root of a function g is a function f satisfying f(f(x)) = g(x) for all x. For example, f(x) = 2x2 is a functional square root of g(x) = 8x4.

a. Debt
b. Point-slope form
c. Total least squares
d. Square function

27. In mathematics, a _____ of a number x is a number r such that r^2 = x, or, in other words, a number r whose square is x. Every non-negative real number x has a unique non-negative _____, called the principal _____, which is denoted with a radical symbol as $\sqrt{x}$, or, using exponent notation, as $x^{1/2}$. For example, the principal _____ of 9 is 3, denoted $\sqrt{9}$ = 3, because 3^2 = 3 × 3 = 9.
   a. Multiplicative inverse
   b. Square root
   c. Double exponential
   d. Hyperbolic functions

28. In computational complexity theory, the complexity class _____ is the union of the classes in the exponential hierarchy.

$$\text{ELEMENTARY} = \text{EXP} \cup \text{2EXP} \cup \text{3EXP} \cup \cdots$$
$$= \text{DTIME}(2^n) \cup \text{DTIME}(2^{2^n}) \cup \text{DTIME}(2^{2^{2^n}}) \cup \cdots$$

The name was coined by Laszlo Kalmar, in the context of recursive functions and undecidability; most problems in it are far from _____. Some natural recursive problems lie outside _____, and are thus NONELEMENTARY.

   a. A chemical equation
   b. Elementary
   c. A posteriori
   d. A Mathematical Theory of Communication

29. In mathematics, an _____ is a function built from a finite number of exponentials, logarithms, constants, one variable, and roots of equations through composition and combinations using the four elementary operations (+ - × ÷.) The trigonometric functions and their inverses are assumed to be included in the _____s by using complex variables and the relations between the trigonometric functions and the exponential and logarithm functions.

_____s are considered a subset of special functions.

a. A Mathematical Theory of Communication
b. Elementary Function
c. A posteriori
d. A chemical equation

30. In vascular plants, the _____ is the organ of a plant body that typically lies below the surface of the soil. This is not always the case, however, since a _____ can also be aerial (that is, growing above the ground) or aerating (that is, growing up above the ground or especially above water.) Furthermore, a stem normally occurring below ground is not exceptional either

a. 1-center problem
b. 120-cell
c. 2-3 heap
d. Root

31. In mathematics, the _____s may be described informally in several different ways. The _____s include both rational numbers, such as 42 and −23/129, and irrational numbers, such as pi and the square root of two; or, a _____ can be given by an infinite decimal representation, such as 2.4871773339...., where the digits continue in some way; or, the _____s may be thought of as points on an infinitely long number line.

These descriptions of the _____s, while intuitively accessible, are not sufficiently rigorous for the purposes of pure mathematics.

a. Tally marks
b. Real number
c. Minkowski distance
d. Pre-algebra

32. _____ is the interpreting of the meaning of a text and the subsequent production of an equivalent text, likewise called a '_____,' that communicates the same message in another language. The text to be translated is called the 'source text,' and the language that it is to be translated into is called the 'target language'; the final product is sometimes called the 'target text.'

_____ must take into account constraints that include context, the rules of grammar of the two languages, their writing conventions, and their idioms. A common misconception is that there exists a simple word-for-word correspondence between any two languages, and that _____ is a straightforward mechanical process; such a word-for-word _____, however, cannot take into account context, grammar, conventions, and idioms.

a. 2-3 heap
b. 120-cell
c. 1-center problem
d. Translation

33. In function graphing, a _____ is a related graph which, for every point (x, y); has a y value which differs from another graph, by exactly some constant c. For example, the antiderivatives of a family are _____s of each other.
  a. Parallel postulate
  b. Central angle
  c. Complementary angles
  d. Vertical translation

34. _____, also sometimes known as standard form or as exponential notation, is a way of writing numbers that accommodates values too large or small to be conveniently written in standard decimal notation. _____ has a number of useful properties and is often favored by scientists, mathematicians and engineers, who work with such numbers.

In _____, numbers are written in the form:

$$a \times 10^b$$

  a. Scientific notation
  b. Leading zero
  c. 1-center problem
  d. Radix point

35. _____ is used to describe the steepness, incline, gradient, or grade of a straight line. A higher _____ value indicates a steeper incline. The _____ is defined as the ratio of the 'rise' divided by the 'run' between two points on a line, or in other words, the ratio of the altitude change to the horizontal distance between any two points on the line.
  a. Number line
  b. Cognitively Guided Instruction
  c. Point plotting
  d. Slope

36. _____ is a form where m is the slope of the line and b is the y-intercept, which is the y-coordinate of the point where the line crosses the y axis. This can be seen by letting x = 0, which immediately gives y = b.

a. Slope-intercept form
b. Separable extension
c. Dynamical system
d. Commutative law

37. The _____ expresses the fact that the difference in the y coordinate between two points on a line that is, y − y1 is proportional to the difference in the x coordinate that is, x − x1. The proportionality constant is m (the slope of the line.
   a. Cobb-Douglas
   b. Square function
   c. Rubin Causal Model
   d. Point-slope form

38. In mathematics, the point $\tilde{\mathbf{x}} \in \mathbb{R}^n$ is an _____ for the differential equation

$$\frac{d\mathbf{x}}{dt} = \mathbf{f}(t, \mathbf{x})$$

if $\mathbf{f}(t, \tilde{\mathbf{x}}) = 0$ for all t.

Similarly, the point $\tilde{\mathbf{x}} \in \mathbb{R}^n$ is an _____ for the difference equation

$$\mathbf{x}_{k+1} = \mathbf{f}(k, \mathbf{x}_k)$$

if $\mathbf{f}(k, \tilde{\mathbf{x}}) = \tilde{\mathbf{x}}$ for $k = 0, 1, 2, \ldots$.

Equilibria can be classified by looking at the signs of the eigenvalues of the linearization of the equations about the equilibria.

   a. Equilibrium point
   b. Algorithm design
   c. Unitary transformation
   d. Uniform algebra

39. _____ is an economic model describing effects on price and quantity in a market. It predicts that in a competitive market, price will function to equalize the quantity demanded by consumers, and the quantity supplied by producers, resulting in an economic equilibrium of price and quantity. The model incorporates other factors changing equilibrium as a shift of demand and/or supply.

Chapter 1. A Beginning Library of Elementary Functions

a. Supply and demand
b. Cross price elasticity of demand
c. Marginal rate of substitution
d. 1-center problem

40. In abstract algebra, a module S over a ring R is called _____ or irreducible if it is not the zero module 0 and if its only submodules are 0 and S. Understanding the _____ modules over a ring is usually helpful because these modules form the 'building blocks' of all other modules in a certain sense.

Abelian groups are the same as Z-modules.

a. Basis
b. Simple
c. Derivation
d. Harmonic series

41. _____ is a fee, paid on borrowed capital. Assets lent include money, shares, consumer goods through hire purchase, major assets such as aircraft, and even entire factories in finance lease arrangements. The _____ is calculated upon the value of the assets in the same manner as upon money.

a. Interest sensitivity gap
b. Interest expense
c. A Mathematical Theory of Communication
d. Interest

42. _____ is a term used in accounting, economics and finance to spread the cost of an asset over the span of several years.

In simple words we can say that _____ is the reduction in the value of an asset due to usage, passage of time, wear and tear, technological outdating or obsolescence, depletion or other such factors.

In accounting, _____ is a term used to describe any method of attributing the historical or purchase cost of an asset across its useful life, roughly corresponding to normal wear and tear.

a. Gross sales
b. Depreciation
c. 120-cell
d. 1-center problem

Chapter 1. A Beginning Library of Elementary Functions 13

43. In signal processing, the _____ E_s of a continuous-time signal x

$$E_s = \langle x(t), x(t) \rangle = \int_{-\infty}^{\infty} |x(t)|^2 dt$$

_____ in this context is not, strictly speaking, the same as the conventional notion of _____ in physics and the other sciences. The two concepts are, however, closely related, and it is possible to convert from one to the other:

$$E = \frac{E_s}{Z} = \frac{1}{Z} \int_{-\infty}^{\infty} |x(t)|^2 dt$$

where Z represents the magnitude, in appropriate units of measure, of the load driven by the signal.

For example, if x

  a. Essential bandwidth
  b. Audio signal processing
  c. Emphasis
  d. Energy

44. In mathematics, the _____ is a conic section, the intersection of a right circular conical surface and a plane parallel to a generating straight line of that surface. Given a point and a line that lie in a plane, the locus of points in that plane that are equidistant to them is a _____.

A particular case arises when the plane is tangent to the conical surface of a circle.

  a. Directrix
  b. Dandelin sphere
  c. Matrix representation of conic sections
  d. Parabola

45. A quadratic equation with real solutions, called roots, which may be real or complex, is given by the _____: $x = \frac{-b \pm \sqrt{b^2 - 4ac}}{2a}$.

  a. Differential Algebra
  b. Parametric continuity
  c. Quotient
  d. Quadratic formula

46. In mathematics and in the sciences, a _____ (plural: _____e, formulæ or _____s) is a concise way of expressing information symbolically (as in a mathematical or chemical _____), or a general relationship between quantities. One of many famous _____e is Albert Einstein's E = mc² (see special relativity

In mathematics, a _____ is a key to solve an equation with variables. For example, the problem of determining the volume of a sphere is one that requires a significant amount of integral calculus to solve.

   a. 1-center problem
   b. Formula
   c. 120-cell
   d. 2-3 heap

47. In geometry, a _____ is a special kind of point, usually a corner of a polygon, polyhedron, or higher dimensional polytope. In the geometry of curves a _____ is a point of where the first derivative of curvature is zero. In graph theory, a _____ is the fundamental unit out of which graphs are formed
   a. Duality
   b. Vertex
   c. Dini
   d. Crib

48. In economics, specifically cost accounting, the _____ is the point at which cost or expenses and revenue are equal: there is no net loss or gain, and one has 'broken even'. Therefore has not made a profit or a loss.

In the linear Cost-Volume-Profit Analysis model, the _____ can be directly computed in terms of Total Revenue and Total Costs as:

$$\begin{aligned} TR &= TC \\ P \times X &= TFC + V \times X \\ P \times X - V \times X &= TFC \\ (P - V) \times X &= TFC \\ X &= \frac{TFC}{P - V} \end{aligned}$$

where:

- TFC is Total Fixed Costs,
- P is Unit Sale Price, and
- V is Unit Variable Cost.

The _____ can alternatively be computed as the point where Contribution equals Fixed Costs.

The quantity $(P - V)$ is of interest in its own right, and is called the Unit Contribution Margin: it is the marginal profit per unit, or alternatively the portion of each sale that contributes to Fixed Costs. Thus the _____ can be more simply computed as the point where Total Contribution = Total Fixed Cost:

$$\text{Total Contribution} = \text{Total Fixed Costs}$$
$$\text{Unit Contribution} \times \text{Number of Units} = \text{Total Fixed Costs}$$
$$\text{Number of Units} = \frac{\text{Total Fixed Costs}}{\text{Unit Contribution}}$$

In currency units to reach break-even, one can use the above calculation and multiply by Price, or equivalently use the

$$\text{Break-even(in Sales)} = \frac{\text{Fixed Costs}}{C/P}.$$

Contribution Margin Ratio to compute it as:

R=C Where R is revenue generated C is cost incurred.

a. Small numbers game
b. Break-even point
c. 120-cell
d. 1-center problem

49. _____ is the flow of blood in the cardiovascular system.

It can be calculated by dividing the vascular resistance into the pressure gradient.

Mathematically, _____ is described by Darcy's law (which can be viewed as the fluid equivalent of Ohm's law) and approximately by Hagen-Poiseuille equation.

a. 2-3 heap
b. 120-cell
c. Blood flow
d. 1-center problem

50. _____ is the concept of adding accumulated interest back to the principal, so that interest is earned on interest from that moment on. The act of declaring interest to be principal is called compounding. A loan, for example, may have its interest compounded every month: in this case, a loan with $100 principal and 1% interest per month would have a balance of $101 at the end of the first month.
  a. Net interest margin
  b. Net interest margin securities
  c. Retained interest
  d. Compound interest

51. In statistics, _____ is a form of regression analysis in which the relationship between one or more independent variables and another variable, called dependent variable, is modeled by a least squares function, called _____ equation. This function is a linear combination of one or more model parameters, called regression coefficients. A _____ equation with one independent variable represents a straight line.
  a. Percentile rank
  b. Random variables
  c. Kurtosis
  d. Linear regression

52. The _____ fallacy is an informal fallacy. It ascribes cause where none exists. The flaw is failing to account for natural fluctuations.
  a. Depth
  b. Degrees of freedom
  c. Differential
  d. Regression

53. In statistics, _____ is a collective name for techniques for the modeling and analysis of numerical data consisting of values of a dependent variable and of one or more independent variables. The dependent variable in the regression equation is modeled as a function of the independent variables, corresponding parameters, and an error term. The error term is treated as a random variable.

a. 1-center problem
b. 120-cell
c. 2-3 heap
d. Regression analysis

Chapter 2. Additional Elementary Functions

1. In mathematics, especially in the area of abstract algebra known as ring theory, a _____ is a ring with 0 ≠ 1 such that ab = 0 implies that either a = 0 or b = 0. That is, it is a nontrivial ring without left or right zero divisors. A commutative _____ is called an integral _____.
    a. Left primitive ring
    b. Simple ring
    c. Modular representation theory
    d. Domain

2. In mathematics, a _____ is an expression constructed from variables and constants, using the operations of addition, subtraction, multiplication, and constant non-negative whole number exponents. For example, $x^2 - 4x + 7$ is a _____, but $x^2 - 4/x + 7x^{3/2}$ is not, because its second term involves division by the variable x and also because its third term contains an exponent that is not a whole number.

    _____s are one of the most important concepts in algebra and throughout mathematics and science.

    a. Polynomial
    b. Semifield
    c. Coimage
    d. Group extension

3. In probability theory, a probability distribution is called _____ if its cumulative distribution function is _____. That is equivalent to saying that for random variables X with the distribution in question, Pr[X = a] = 0 for all real numbers a. If the distribution of X is _____ then X is called a _____ random variable.
    a. Continuous
    b. Concatenated codes
    c. Continuous phase modulation
    d. Conull set

4. In calculus, a function f defined on a subset of the real numbers with real values is called monotonic (also monotonically increasing or non-_____), if for all x and y such that x ≤ y one has f(x) ≤ f(y), so f preserves the order. In layman's terms, the sign of the slope is always positive (the curve tending upwards) or zero (i.e., non-_____, or asymptotic, or depicted as a horizontal, flat line) Likewise, a function is called monotonically _____ (non-increasing) if, whenever x ≤ y, then f(x) ≥ f(y), so it reverses the order.
    a. Dual pair
    b. Decreasing
    c. Circular convolution
    d. Tensor product of Hilbert spaces

Chapter 2. Additional Elementary Functions

5. The mathematical concept of a _____ expresses the intuitive idea of deterministic dependence between two quantities, one of which is viewed as primary and the other as secondary. A _____ then is a way to associate a unique output for each input of a specified type, for example, a real number or an element of a given set.
    a. Function
    b. Grill
    c. Going up
    d. Coherent

6. In mathematics, the _____ of a real number is its numerical value without regard to its sign. So, for example, 3 is the _____ of both 3 and −3.

    The _____ of a number a is denoted by $|a|$.

    Generalizations of the _____ for real numbers occur in a wide variety of mathematical settings.

    a. Area hyperbolic functions
    b. Absolute value
    c. A chemical equation
    d. A Mathematical Theory of Communication

7. In mathematics, a _____ is a function for which, intuitively, small changes in the input result in small changes in the output. Otherwise, a function is said to be discontinuous. A _____ with a continuous inverse function is called bicontinuous.
    a. Contraction mapping
    b. Charles's Law
    c. Beth numbers
    d. Continuous Function

8. In vascular plants, the _____ is the organ of a plant body that typically lies below the surface of the soil. This is not always the case, however, since a _____ can also be aerial (that is, growing above the ground) or aerating (that is, growing up above the ground or especially above water.) Furthermore, a stem normally occurring below ground is not exceptional either
    a. 1-center problem
    b. Root
    c. 120-cell
    d. 2-3 heap

9. In mathematics, a _____ is a constant multiplicative factor of a certain object. For example, in the expression $9x^2$, the _____ of x^2 is 9.

The object can be such things as a variable, a vector, a function, etc.

   a. Stability radius
   b. Multivariate division algorithm
   c. Fibonacci polynomials
   d. Coefficient

10. In the physical sciences, _____ is a measurement of the gravitational force acting on an object. Near the surface of the Earth, the acceleration due to gravity is approximately constant; this means that an object's _____ is roughly proportional to its mass.

In commerce and in many other applications, _____ means the same as mass as that term is used in physics.

   a. 1-center problem
   b. 120-cell
   c. 2-3 heap
   d. Weight

11. _____ was the Allied codename for any of several German teleprinter stream ciphers used during World War II. Enciphered teleprinter traffic was used between German High Command and Army Group commanders in the field, so its intelligence value was of the highest strategic value to the Allies. This traffic normally passed over landlines, but as German forces extended their reach out of western Europe, they had to resort to wireless transmission.
   a. Colossus
   b. Function
   c. Divide and conquer
   d. Fish

12. An _____ of a real-valued function $y = f(x)$ is a curve which describes the behavior of f as either x or y tends to infinity.

In other words, as one moves along the graph of $f(x)$ in some direction, the distance between it and the _____ eventually becomes smaller than any distance that one may specify.

If a curve A has the curve B as an _____, one says that A is asymptotic to B. Similarly B is asymptotic to A, so A and B are called asymptotic.

Chapter 2. Additional Elementary Functions

a. Asymptote
b. Isoperimetric dimension
c. Infinite product
d. Improper integral

13. Suppose f is a function. Then the line y = a is a _____ for f if

$$\lim_{x \to \infty} f(x) = a \quad \text{or} \quad \lim_{x \to -\infty} f(x) = a.$$

Intuitively, this means that f(x) can be made as close as desired to a by making x big enough. How big is big enough depends on how close one wishes to make f(x) to a.

a. 2-3 heap
b. Horizontal asymptote
c. 1-center problem
d. 120-cell

14. In mathematics, an _____, or central tendency of a data set refers to a measure of the 'middle' or 'expected' value of the data set. There are many different descriptive statistics that can be chosen as a measurement of the central tendency of the data items.

An _____ is a single value that is meant to typify a list of values.

a. A Mathematical Theory of Communication
b. Average
c. A posteriori
d. A chemical equation

15. In economics, _____ is equal to total cost divided by the number of goods produced Quantity-Q. It is also equal to the sum of average variable costs total variable costs divided by Q plus average fixed costs total fixed costs divided by Q. _____s may be dependent on the time period considered increasing production may be expensive or impossible in the short term, for example. _____s affect the supply curve and are a fundamental component of supply and demand.

a. Equity
b. Average cost
c. Extreme value theorem
d. Uncertainty quantification

Chapter 2. Additional Elementary Functions

16. In economics, business, retail, and accounting, a _____ is the value of money that has been used up to produce something, and hence is not available for use anymore. In business, the _____ may be one of acquisition, in which case the amount of money expended to acquire it is counted as _____. In this case, money is the input that is gone in order to acquire the thing.

   a. 120-cell
   b. 2-3 heap
   c. 1-center problem
   d. Cost

17. In computational complexity theory, an algorithm is said to take _____ if the asymptotic upper bound for the time it requires is proportional to the size of the input, which is usually denoted n.

Informally spoken, the running time increases linearly with the size of the input. For example, a procedure that adds up all elements of a list requires time proportional to the length of the list.

   a. Constructible function
   b. Linear time
   c. Time-constructible function
   d. Truth table reduction

18. In mathematics, the point $\tilde{x} \in \mathbb{R}^n$ is an _____ for the differential equation

$$\frac{d\mathbf{x}}{dt} = \mathbf{f}(t, \mathbf{x})$$

if $\mathbf{f}(t, \tilde{\mathbf{x}}) = 0$ for all t.

Similarly, the point $\tilde{x} \in \mathbb{R}^n$ is an _____ for the difference equation

$$\mathbf{x}_{k+1} = \mathbf{f}(k, \mathbf{x}_k)$$

if $\mathbf{f}(k, \tilde{\mathbf{x}}) = \tilde{\mathbf{x}}$ for $k = 0, 1, 2, \ldots$.

Equilibria can be classified by looking at the signs of the eigenvalues of the linearization of the equations about the equilibria.

a. Uniform algebra
b. Algorithm design
c. Unitary transformation
d. Equilibrium point

19. In mathematics and computer science, _____ (also base-16, hexa or base, of 16. It uses sixteen distinct symbols, most often the symbols 0-9 to represent values zero to nine, and A, B, C, D, E, F (or a through f) to represent values ten to fifteen.

Its primary use is as a human friendly representation of binary coded values, so it is often used in digital electronics and computer engineering.

a. Tetradecimal
b. Radix
c. Factoradic
d. Hexadecimal

20. In descriptive statistics, the _____ is the length of the smallest interval which contains all the data. It is calculated by subtracting the smallest observations from the greatest and provides an indication of statistical dispersion.

It is measured in the same units as the data.

a. Class
b. Kernel
c. Bandwidth
d. Range

21. The _____ (helpÂ·) (singular: bacterium) are a large group of unicellular microorganisms. Typically a few micrometres in length, _____ have a wide range of shapes, ranging from spheres to rods and spirals. _____ are ubiquitous in every habitat on Earth, growing in soil, acidic hot springs, radioactive waste, water, and deep in the Earth's crust, as well as in organic matter and the live bodies of plants and animals.
a. ROT13
b. Data Encryption Standard
c. Vampire
d. Bacteria

Chapter 2. Additional Elementary Functions

22. The _____ is a function in mathematics. The application of this function to a value x is written as ex. Equivalently, this can be written in the form e^x, where e is a mathematical constant, the base of the natural logarithm, which equals approximately 2.718281828, and is also known as Euler's number.

   a. A Mathematical Theory of Communication
   b. Area hyperbolic functions
   c. A chemical equation
   d. Exponential function

23. _____ occurs when the growth rate of a mathematical function is proportional to the function's current value. In the case of a discrete domain of definition with equal intervals it is also called geometric growth or geometric decay.

With _____ of a positive value its rate of increase steadily increases, or in the case of exponential decay, its rate of decrease steadily decreases.

   a. A Mathematical Theory of Communication
   b. A chemical equation
   c. Exponential growth
   d. A posteriori

24. A quantity is said to be subject to _____ if it decreases at a rate proportional to its value. Symbolically, this can be expressed as the following differential equation, where N is the quantity and λ is a positive number called the decay constant.

$$\frac{dN}{dt} = -\lambda N.$$

The solution to this equation is:

$$N(t) = N_0 e^{-\lambda t}.$$

Here is the quantity at time t, and N_0 = N is the quantity, at time t = 0.

   a. Exponential integral
   b. Exponential decay
   c. Exponential formula
   d. Exponentiating by squaring

25. _____ is a term used in accounting, economics and finance to spread the cost of an asset over the span of several years.

In simple words we can say that _____ is the reduction in the value of an asset due to usage, passage of time, wear and tear, technological outdating or obsolescence, depletion or other such factors.

In accounting, _____ is a term used to describe any method of attributing the historical or purchase cost of an asset across its useful life, roughly corresponding to normal wear and tear.

a. 1-center problem
b. Gross sales
c. 120-cell
d. Depreciation

26. _____ is a fee, paid on borrowed capital. Assets lent include money, shares, consumer goods through hire purchase, major assets such as aircraft, and even entire factories in finance lease arrangements. The _____ is calculated upon the value of the assets in the same manner as upon money.
a. Interest expense
b. Interest sensitivity gap
c. A Mathematical Theory of Communication
d. Interest

27. _____ is the concept of adding accumulated interest back to the principal, so that interest is earned on interest from that moment on. The act of declaring interest to be principal is called compounding. A loan, for example, may have its interest compounded every month: in this case, a loan with $100 principal and 1% interest per month would have a balance of $101 at the end of the first month.
a. Retained interest
b. Net interest margin
c. Net interest margin securities
d. Compound interest

28. _____ is the change in population over time, and can be quantified as the change in the number of individuals in a population using 'per unit time' for measurement. The term _____ can technically refer to any species, but almost always refers to humans, and it is often used informally for the more specific demographic term _____ rate, and is often used to refer specifically to the growth of the population of the world.

Simple models of _____ include the Malthusian Growth Model and the logistic model.

a. 120-cell
b. Population growth
c. Population dynamics
d. 1-center problem

29. In mathematics, the concept of a _____ tries to capture the intuitive idea of a geometrical one-dimensional and continuous object. A simple example is the circle. In everyday use of the term '_____', a straight line is not curved, but in mathematical parlance _____s include straight lines and line segments.
   a. Kappa curve
   b. Quadrifolium
   c. Negative pedal curve
   d. Curve

30. _____ is the average number of years of life remaining at a given age. _____ is heavily dependent on the criteria used to select the group. In countries with high infant mortality rates, the _____ at birth is highly sensitive to the rate of death in the first few years of life.
   a. Life expectancy
   b. Abraham Sinkov
   c. Agnes Meyer Driscoll
   d. Adi Shamir

31. In mathematics, the _____ of a number n is the number that, when added to n, yields zero. The _____ of n is denoted −n. For example, 7 is −7, because 7 + (−7) = 0, and the _____ of −0.3 is 0.3, because −0.3 + 0.3 = 0.
   a. Associativity
   b. Additive inverse
   c. Arity
   d. Algebraic structure

32. An _____ is a function which does the reverse of a given function.
   a. Empty function
   b. A Mathematical Theory of Communication
   c. Empty set
   d. Inverse function

33. An injective function is called an injection, and is also said to be a _____ (not to be confused with one-to-one correspondence, i.e. a bijective function.)

A function f that is not injective is sometimes called many-to-one. (However, this terminology is also sometimes used to mean 'single-valued', i.e. each argument is mapped to at most one value.)

a. A posteriori
b. One-to-one function
c. A chemical equation
d. A Mathematical Theory of Communication

34. The _____ is the logarithm with base 10. It is also known as the decadic logarithm, named after its base. It is indicated by $\log_{10}$

a. Common logarithm
b. 1-center problem
c. Logarithmic growth
d. Natural logarithm

35. The _____, formerly known as the hyperbolic logarithm, is the logarithm to the base e, where e is an irrational constant approximately equal to 2.718 281 828. It is also sometimes referred to as the Napierian logarithm, although the original meaning of this term is slightly different. In simple terms, the _____ of a number x is the power to which e would have to be raised to equal x -- for example the natural log of e itself is 1 because e^1 = e, while the _____ of 1 would be 0, since e^0 = 1.

a. Logarithmic identities
b. Logarithmic growth
c. 1-center problem
d. Natural logarithm

36. A _____ is a device for performing mathematical calculations, distinguished from a computer by having a limited problem solving ability and an interface optimized for interactive calculation rather than programming. _____s can be hardware or software, and mechanical or electronic, and are often built into devices such as PDAs or mobile phones.

Modern electronic _____s are generally small, digital, and usually inexpensive.

a. 120-cell
b. 2-3 heap
c. Calculator
d. 1-center problem

Chapter 2. Additional Elementary Functions

37. In mathematics, the _____ of a number to a given base is the power or exponent to which the base must be raised in order to produce the number.

For example, the _____ of 1000 to the base 10 is 3, because 3 is how many 10s one must multiply to get 1000: thus 10 × 10 × 10 = 1000; the base-2 _____ of 32 is 5 because 5 is how many 2s one must multiply to get 32: thus 2 × 2 × 2 × 2 × 2 = 32. In the language of exponents: 10^3 = 1000, so $\log_{10} 1000$ = 3, and 2^5 = 32, so $\log_2 32$ = 5.

a. 2-3 heap
b. 120-cell
c. 1-center problem
d. Logarithm

38. The _____ is the period of time required for a quantity to double in size or value.
a. Stretched exponential function
b. Zenzizenzizenzic
c. Doubling time
d. Power law

39. In mathematics and in the sciences, a _____ (plural: _____ e, formulæ or _____ s) is a concise way of expressing information symbolically (as in a mathematical or chemical _____), or a general relationship between quantities. One of many famous _____ e is Albert Einstein's E = mc² (see special relativity

In mathematics, a _____ is a key to solve an equation with variables. For example, the problem of determining the volume of a sphere is one that requires a significant amount of integral calculus to solve.

a. 120-cell
b. 2-3 heap
c. Formula
d. 1-center problem

40. _____ is an economic model describing effects on price and quantity in a market. It predicts that in a competitive market, price will function to equalize the quantity demanded by consumers, and the quantity supplied by producers, resulting in an economic equilibrium of price and quantity. The model incorporates other factors changing equilibrium as a shift of demand and/or supply.

Chapter 2. Additional Elementary Functions

a. Supply and demand
b. Marginal rate of substitution
c. 1-center problem
d. Cross price elasticity of demand

41. _____ is the assisted transmission of signals over a distance for the purpose of communication. In earlier times, this may have involved the use of smoke signals, drums, semaphore, flags, Morse Code, or heliograph. In modern times, _____ typically involves the use of electronic transmitters such as the telephone, television, radio or computer.
   a. 1-center problem
   b. Telecommunication
   c. 2-3 heap
   d. 120-cell

42. The _____ fallacy is an informal fallacy. It ascribes cause where none exists. The flaw is failing to account for natural fluctuations.
   a. Depth
   b. Degrees of freedom
   c. Regression
   d. Differential

43. In statistics, _____ is a collective name for techniques for the modeling and analysis of numerical data consisting of values of a dependent variable and of one or more independent variables. The dependent variable in the regression equation is modeled as a function of the independent variables, corresponding parameters, and an error term. The error term is treated as a random variable.
   a. 1-center problem
   b. Regression analysis
   c. 120-cell
   d. 2-3 heap

44. The method of _____ or ordinary _____ is used to solve overdetermined systems. _____ is often applied in statistical contexts, particularly regression analysis.

_____ can be interpreted as a method of fitting data.

a. System equivalence
b. Rata Die
c. Non-linear least squares
d. Least squares

45. In statistics, _____ is a form of regression analysis in which the relationship between one or more independent variables and another variable, called dependent variable, is modeled by a least squares function, called _____ equation. This function is a linear combination of one or more model parameters, called regression coefficients. A _____ equation with one independent variable represents a straight line.
   a. Random variables
   b. Kurtosis
   c. Linear regression
   d. Percentile rank

Chapter 3. Mathematics of Finance 31

1. _____ is a fee, paid on borrowed capital. Assets lent include money, shares, consumer goods through hire purchase, major assets such as aircraft, and even entire factories in finance lease arrangements. The _____ is calculated upon the value of the assets in the same manner as upon money.
    a. Interest
    b. Interest sensitivity gap
    c. Interest expense
    d. A Mathematical Theory of Communication

2. In abstract algebra, a module S over a ring R is called _____ or irreducible if it is not the zero module 0 and if its only submodules are 0 and S. Understanding the _____ modules over a ring is usually helpful because these modules form the 'building blocks' of all other modules in a certain sense.

Abelian groups are the same as Z-modules.

    a. Harmonic series
    b. Derivation
    c. Basis
    d. Simple

3. _____ is the concept of adding accumulated interest back to the principal, so that interest is earned on interest from that moment on. The act of declaring interest to be principal is called compounding. A loan, for example, may have its interest compounded every month: in this case, a loan with $100 principal and 1% interest per month would have a balance of $101 at the end of the first month.
    a. Retained interest
    b. Compound interest
    c. Net interest margin securities
    d. Net interest margin

4. In mathematics, a _____ is a number that can be expressed as an integral of an algebraic function over an algebraic domain. Kontsevich and Zagier define a _____ as a complex number whose real and imaginary parts are values of absolutely convergent integrals of rational functions with rational coefficients, over domains in given by polynomial inequalities with rational coefficients.
    a. Boussinesq approximation
    b. Disk
    c. Closeness
    d. Period

5. In computational complexity theory, an algorithm is said to take _____ if the asymptotic upper bound for the time it requires is proportional to the size of the input, which is usually denoted n.

Informally spoken, the running time increases linearly with the size of the input. For example, a procedure that adds up all elements of a list requires time proportional to the length of the list.

a. Linear time
b. Truth table reduction
c. Constructible function
d. Time-constructible function

6.

A _____ is an official document affirming some fact. For example, a birth _____ or death _____ testifies to basic facts regarding a person's birth or death. A _____ may also certify that a person has received specific education or has passed a test, and is considered below the standard of an academic degree.

a. Certificate
b. 1-center problem
c. 2-3 heap
d. 120-cell

7. _____ expresses an annual rate of interest taking into account the effect of compounding, usually for deposit or investment products. It is analogous to the Annual percentage rate, which is used for loans. In some jurisdictions, the use and definition of _____ may be regulated by a government agency, in which case it would generally be capitalized.

a. Annual percentage yield
b. A Mathematical Theory of Communication
c. A posteriori
d. A chemical equation

8. In mathematics, a _____ is a way of expressing a number as a fraction of 100. It is often denoted using the percent sign, '%'. For example, 45% is equal to 45 / 100, or 0.45.

a. Subtrahend
b. Percentage
c. Least common multiple
d. Lowest common denominator

9. The _____ is the period of time required for a quantity to double in size or value.

Chapter 3. Mathematics of Finance 33

a. Stretched exponential function
b. Doubling time
c. Power law
d. Zenzizenzizenzic

10. In economics, business, retail, and accounting, a _____ is the value of money that has been used up to produce something, and hence is not available for use anymore. In business, the _____ may be one of acquisition, in which case the amount of money expended to acquire it is counted as _____. In this case, money is the input that is gone in order to acquire the thing.

a. 120-cell
b. 2-3 heap
c. 1-center problem
d. Cost

11. The term _____ refers to the central sense organ complex, for those animals that have one, normally on the ventral surface of the head and can depending on the definition in the human case, include the hair, forehead, eyebrow, eyes, nose, ears, cheeks, mouth, lips, philtrum, teeth, skin, and chin. The _____ has uses of expression, appearance, and identity amongst others.It also has different senses like smelling, tasting, hearing, and seeing.

Caricatures often exaggerate facial features to make a _____ more easily recognized in association with a pronounced portion of the _____ of the individual in question--for example, a caricature of Osama bin Laden might focus on his facial hair and nose; a caricature of George W. Bush might enlarge his ears to the size of an elephant¢s; a caricature of Jay Leno may pronounce his head and chin; and a caricature of Mick Jagger might enlarge his lips.

a. 1-center problem
b. Face
c. 120-cell
d. 2-3 heap

12. In financial accounting, a _____ or statement of financial position is a summary of a person's or organization's balances. Assets, liabilities and ownership equity are listed as of a specific date, such as the end of its financial year. A _____ is often described as a snapshot of a company's financial condition.

a. Balance sheet
b. 2-3 heap
c. 120-cell
d. 1-center problem

13. _____ or amortisation is the process of decreasing an amount over a period of time. The word comes from Middle English amortisen to kill, alienate in mortmain, from Anglo-French amorteser, alteration of amortir, from Vulgar Latin admortire to kill, from Latin ad- + mort-, mors death. Particular instances of the term include:

- _____, the allocation of a lump sum amount to different time periods, particularly for loans and other forms of finance, including related interest or other finance charges.
    - _____ schedule, a table detailing each periodic payment on a loan, as generated by an _____ calculator.
    - Negative _____, an _____ schedule where the loan amount actually increases through not paying the full interest
- Amortized analysis, analyzing the execution cost of algorithms over a sequence of operations.
- _____ of capital expenditures of certain assets under accounting rules, particularly intangible assets, in a manner analogous to depreciation.
- _____

_____ is also used in the context of zoning regulations and describes the time in which a property owner has to relocate when the property's use constitutes a preexisting nonconforming use under zoning regulations.

- Depreciation

a. ISAAC
b. Origin
c. Amortization
d. Identity

14. A _____ is the transfer of an interest in property (or in law the equivalent - a charge) to a lender as a security for a debt - usually a loan of money. While a _____ in itself is not a debt, it is lender's security for a debt. It is a transfer of an interest in land (or the equivalent), from the owner to the _____ lender, on the condition that this interest will be returned to the owner of the real estate when the terms of the _____ have been satisfied or performed.
a. 2-3 heap
b. 120-cell
c. Mortgage
d. 1-center problem

15. _____ is the concept or idea of fairness in economics, particularly as to taxation or welfare economics.
a. Interval
b. Union
c. Event
d. Equity

Chapter 3. Mathematics of Finance

16. The _____ (IRR) is a capital budgeting metric used by firms to decide whether they should make investments. It is an indicator of the efficiency or quality of an investment, as opposed to net present value (NPV), which indicates value or magnitude.

The IRR is the annualized effective compounded return rate which can be earned on the invested capital.

    a. Enterprise value
    b. Internal rate of return
    c. Exotic option
    d. Intertemporal CAPM

17. In finance, _____ rate of profit or sometimes just return, is the ratio of money gained or lost on an investment relative to the amount of money invested. The amount of money gained or lost may be referred to as interest, profit/loss, gain/loss, or net income/loss. The money invested may be referred to as the asset, capital, principal, or the cost basis of the investment.
    a. P/E ratio
    b. Return on equity
    c. Rate of return
    d. 1-center problem

Chapter 4. Systems of Linear Equations; Matrices

1. A _____ is an algebraic equation in which each term is either a constant or the product of a constant and a single variable. _____s can have one, two, three or more variables.

_____s occur with great regularity in applied mathematics.

    a. Quadratic equation
    b. Quartic equation
    c. Linear equation
    d. Difference of two squares

2. In logic, a theory is _____ if it does not contain a contradiction. The lack of contradiction can be defined in either semantic or syntactic terms. The semantic definition states that a theory is _____ if it has a model; this is the sense used in traditional Aristotelian logic, although in contemporary mathematical logic the term satisfiable is used instead.
    a. Logic
    b. Second-order logic
    c. First-order logic
    d. Consistent

3. In the study of metric spaces in mathematics, there are various notions of two metrics on the same underlying space being 'the same', or _____.

In the following, M will denote a non-empty set and d_1 and d_2 will denote two metrics on M.

The two metrics d_1 and d_2 are said to be topologically _____ if they generate the same topology on M.

    a. Equivalent
    b. A posteriori
    c. A Mathematical Theory of Communication
    d. A chemical equation

4. In linear algebra, _____ is a version of Gaussian elimination that puts zeros both above and below each pivot element as it goes from the top row of the given matrix to the bottom. In other words, _____ brings a matrix to reduced row echelon form, whereas Gaussian elimination takes it only as far as row echelon form. Every matrix has a reduced row echelon form, and this algorithm is guaranteed to produce it.
    a. Spheroidal wave functions
    b. Gauss-Jordan elimination
    c. Lax equivalence theorem
    d. Conservation form

Chapter 4. Systems of Linear Equations; Matrices

5. _____ is an economic model describing effects on price and quantity in a market. It predicts that in a competitive market, price will function to equalize the quantity demanded by consumers, and the quantity supplied by producers, resulting in an economic equilibrium of price and quantity. The model incorporates other factors changing equilibrium as a shift of demand and/or supply.

   a. 1-center problem
   b. Cross price elasticity of demand
   c. Marginal rate of substitution
   d. Supply and demand

6. In mathematics, the point $\tilde{\mathbf{x}} \in \mathbb{R}^n$ is an _____ for the differential equation

$$\frac{d\mathbf{x}}{dt} = \mathbf{f}(t, \mathbf{x})$$

if $\mathbf{f}(t, \tilde{\mathbf{x}}) = 0$ for all t.

Similarly, the point $\tilde{\mathbf{x}} \in \mathbb{R}^n$ is an _____ for the difference equation

$$\mathbf{x}_{k+1} = \mathbf{f}(k, \mathbf{x}_k)$$

if $\mathbf{f}(k, \tilde{\mathbf{x}}) = \tilde{\mathbf{x}}$ for $k = 0, 1, 2, \ldots$.

Equilibria can be classified by looking at the signs of the eigenvalues of the linearization of the equations about the equilibria.

   a. Uniform algebra
   b. Unitary transformation
   c. Algorithm design
   d. Equilibrium point

7. A _____ is any physical or virtual entity of limited availability, or anything used to help one earn a living. In most cases, commercial or even ethic factors require _____ allocation through _____ management. Clean drinking water is a _____ required by all people.

As _____s are very useful, we attach some information value to them.

Chapter 4. Systems of Linear Equations; Matrices

   a. 2-3 heap
   b. 1-center problem
   c. 120-cell
   d. Resource

8. In mathematics, an _____ or member of a set is any one of the distinct objects that make up that set.

Writing A = {1,2,3,4}, means that the _____s of the set A are the numbers 1, 2, 3 and 4. Groups of _____s of A, for example {1,2}, are subsets of A.

   a. Order
   b. Ideal
   c. Universal code
   d. Element

9. In mathematics, a _____ is a rectangular table of elements, which may be numbers or, more generally, any abstract quantities that can be added and multiplied. Matrices are used to describe linear equations, keep track of the coefficients of linear transformations and to record data that depend on multiple parameters. Matrices are described by the field of _____ theory.
   a. Coherent
   b. Double counting
   c. Compression
   d. Matrix

10. In mathematics, _____ is the operation of adding two matrices by adding the corresponding entries together. However, there is another operation which could also be considered as a kind of addition for matrices.

The usual _____ is defined for two matrices of the same dimensions.

   a. Jordan normal form
   b. Spectral theory
   c. Standard basis
   d. Matrix addition

11. In mathematics, an _____ in the sense of ring theory is a subring $\mathcal{O}$ of a ring R that satisfies the conditions

   1. R is a ring which is a finite-dimensional algebra over the rational number field $\mathbb{Q}$
   2. $\mathcal{O}$ spans R over $\mathbb{Q}$, so that $\mathbb{Q}\mathcal{O} = R$, and
   3. $\mathcal{O}$ is a lattice in R.

The third condition can be stated more accurately, in terms of the extension of scalars of R to the real numbers, embedding R in a real vector space. In less formal terms, additively $\mathcal{O}$ should be a free abelian group generated by a basis for R over $\mathbb{Q}$.

The leading example is the case where R is a number field K and $\mathcal{O}$ is its ring of integers. In algebraic number theory there are examples for any K other than the rational field of proper subrings of the ring of integers that are also _____s.

   a. Order
   b. Annihilator
   c. Efficiency
   d. Algebraic

12. In linear algebra, a column vector or _____ is an m × 1 matrix, i.e. a matrix consisting of a single column of m elements.

$$\mathbf{x} = \begin{bmatrix} x_1 \\ x_2 \\ \vdots \\ x_m \end{bmatrix}$$

The transpose of a column vector is a row vector and vice versa.

The set of all column vectors forms a vector space which is the dual space to the set of all row vectors.

   a. Spread of a matrix
   b. Cayley-Hamilton theorem
   c. Column matrix
   d. Split-complex number

13. In linear algebra, a row vector or _____ is a 1 × n matrix, that is, a matrix consisting of a single row:

$$\mathbf{x} = \begin{bmatrix} x_1 & x_2 & \ldots & x_m \end{bmatrix}.$$

The transpose of a row vector is a column vector:

$$\begin{bmatrix} x_1 \\ x_2 \\ \vdots \\ x_m \end{bmatrix} = \begin{bmatrix} x_1 & x_2 & \ldots & x_m \end{bmatrix}^{\mathrm{T}}.$$

The set of all row vectors forms a vector space which is the dual space to the set of all column vectors.

Row vectors are sometimes written using the following non-standard notation:

$$\mathbf{x} = \begin{bmatrix} x_1, x_2, \ldots, x_m \end{bmatrix}.$$

- Matrix multiplication involves the action of multiplying each row vector of one matrix by each column vector of another matrix.

- The dot product of two vectors a and b is equivalent to multiplying the row vector representation of a by the column vector representation of b:

$$\mathbf{a} \cdot \mathbf{b} = \begin{bmatrix} a_1 & a_2 & a_3 \end{bmatrix} \begin{bmatrix} b_1 \\ b_2 \\ b_3 \end{bmatrix}.$$

a. Row matrix
b. Dual vector space
c. Gram-Schmidt process
d. Woodbury matrix identity

14.   In linear algebra, a _____ is a square matrix in which the entries outside the main diagonal are all zero. The diagonal entries themselves may or may not be zero. Thus, the matrix D = with n columns and n rows is diagonal if:

$$d_{i,j} = 0 \text{ if } i \neq j \qquad \forall i, j \in \{1, 2, \ldots, n\}$$

For example, the following matrix is diagonal:

$$\begin{bmatrix} 1 & 0 & 0 \\ 0 & 4 & 0 \\ 0 & 0 & -3 \end{bmatrix}.$$

The term _____ may sometimes refer to a rectangular _____, which is an m-by-n matrix with only the entries of the form $d_{i,i}$ possibly non-zero; for example,

$$\begin{bmatrix} 1 & 0 & 0 \\ 0 & 4 & 0 \\ 0 & 0 & -3 \\ 0 & 0 & 0 \end{bmatrix}, \text{ or } \begin{bmatrix} 1 & 0 & 0 & 0 & 0 \\ 0 & 4 & 0 & 0 & 0 \\ 0 & 0 & -3 & 0 & 0 \end{bmatrix}.$$

a. Hankel matrix
b. Design matrix
c. Transition matrix
d. Diagonal Matrix

15. In linear algebra, the _____ of a matrix is obtained by changing a matrix in some way.

Given the matrices A and B, where:

$$A = \begin{bmatrix} 1 & 3 & 2 \\ 2 & 0 & 1 \\ 5 & 2 & 2 \end{bmatrix}, \quad B = \begin{bmatrix} 4 \\ 3 \\ 1 \end{bmatrix}$$

Then, the _____ is written as:

$$(A|B) = \begin{bmatrix} 1 & 3 & 2 & 4 \\ 2 & 0 & 1 & 3 \\ 5 & 2 & 2 & 1 \end{bmatrix}$$

This is useful when solving systems of linear equations or the _____ may also be used to find the inverse of a matrix by combining it with the identity matrix.

Let C be a square 2×2 matrix where $C = \begin{bmatrix} 1 & 3 \\ -5 & 0 \end{bmatrix}$

To find the inverse of C we create where I is the 2×2 identity matrix.

a. Eigendecomposition
b. Alternating sign matrix
c. Unimodular polynomial matrix
d. Augmented matrix

16. _____ is a branch of mathematics which focuses on the study of matrices. Initially a sub-branch of linear algebra, it has grown to cover subjects related to graph theory, algebra, combinatorics, and statistics as well.

The term matrix was first coined in 1848 by J.J. Sylvester as a name of an array of numbers.

a. Matrix theory
b. Semi-simple operators
c. Segre classification
d. Pairing

17. In statistics, and particularly in econometrics, the _____ of a system of equations is the result of solving the system for the endogenous variables. This gives the latter as a function of the exogenous variables, if any.

Let Y and X be random vectors.

a. Test for structural change
b. Log-linear
c. Dynamic factor
d. Reduced form

18. In mathematics, a _____ is a matrix formed by selecting certain rows and columns from a bigger matrix. That is, as an array, it is cut down to those entries constrained by row and column.

For example

$$\mathbf{A} = \begin{bmatrix} a_{11} & a_{12} & a_{13} & a_{14} \\ a_{21} & a_{22} & a_{23} & a_{24} \\ a_{31} & a_{32} & a_{33} & a_{34} \end{bmatrix}.$$

Then

$$\mathbf{A}[1,2;1,3,4] = \begin{bmatrix} a_{11} & a_{13} & a_{14} \\ a_{21} & a_{23} & a_{24} \end{bmatrix}$$

is a _____ of A formed by rows 1,2 and columns 1,3,4.

   a. Matrix decomposition
   b. Matrix unit
   c. Jordan matrix
   d. Submatrix

19. _____ is an important tool for manufacturing and engineering, where it can have a major impact on the productivity of a process. In manufacturing, the purpose of _____ is to minimize the production time and costs, by telling a production facility what to make, when, with which staff, and on which equipment. Production _____ aims to maximize the efficiency of the operation and reduce costs.
   a. Boolean algebra
   b. Critical point
   c. Crib
   d. Scheduling

20. The mathematical or engineering study of _____, and in particular vehicular _____, is done with the aim of achieving a better understanding of these phenomena and to assist in the reduction of traffic congestion problems.

Attempts to produce a mathematical theory of _____ date back to the 1950s but have so far failed to produce a satisfactory general theory that can be consistently applied to real flow conditions. Current traffic models use a mixture of empirical and theoretical techniques.

a. 120-cell
b. Microscopic traffic flow models
c. Traffic flow
d. 1-center problem

21. In mathematics, _____ is a property that a binary operation can have. It means that, within an expression containing two or more of the same associative operators in a row, the order that the operations are performed does not matter as long as the sequence of the operands is not changed. That is, rearranging the parentheses in such an expression will not change its value.
   a. Associativity
   b. Unital
   c. Idempotence
   d. Algebraically closed

22. In economics, business, retail, and accounting, a _____ is the value of money that has been used up to produce something, and hence is not available for use anymore. In business, the _____ may be one of acquisition, in which case the amount of money expended to acquire it is counted as _____. In this case, money is the input that is gone in order to acquire the thing.
   a. 120-cell
   b. 2-3 heap
   c. 1-center problem
   d. Cost

23. _____ is the mathematical operation of scaling one number by another. It is one of the four basic operations in elementary arithmetic.

_____ is defined for whole numbers in terms of repeated addition; for example, 4 multiplied by 3 can be calculated by adding 3 copies of 4 together:

$$4 + 4 + 4 = 12.$$

_____ of rational numbers and real numbers is defined by systematic generalization of this basic idea.

   a. Least common multiple
   b. The number 0 is even.
   c. Highest common factor
   d. Multiplication

Chapter 4. Systems of Linear Equations; Matrices

24. In the mathematical discipline of linear algebra, a _____ is a special kind of square matrix where the entries either below or above the main diagonal are zero. Because matrix equations with triangular matrices are easier to solve they are very important in numerical analysis. The LU decomposition gives an algorithm to decompose any invertible matrix A into a normed lower triangle matrix L and an upper triangle matrix U.

   a. Successive over-relaxation
   b. Crout matrix decomposition
   c. Rayleigh quotient iteration
   d. Triangular Matrix

25. In mathematics, an _____ is a matrix that shows the relationship between two classes of objects. If the first class is X and the second is Y, the matrix has one row for each element of X and one column for each element of Y. The entry in row x and column y is 1 if x and y are related (called incident in this context) and 0 if they are not.

   a. A posteriori
   b. A chemical equation
   c. A Mathematical Theory of Communication
   d. Incidence matrix

26. _____ consists of 'social relations involving authority or power' and refers to the regulation of a political unit, and to the methods and tactics used to formulate and apply policy.

   Political science (also political studies) is the study of political behavior, and examines the acquisition and application of power. Related areas of study include political philosophy, which seeks a rationale for _____ and an ethic of public behavior, and public administration, which examines the practices of governance.

   a. 120-cell
   b. 1-center problem
   c. 2-3 heap
   d. Politics

27. In game theory, _____ occurs when one strategy is better than another strategy for one player, no matter how that player's opponents may play. Many simple games can be solved using _____. The opposite, intransitivity, occurs in games where one strategy may be better or worse than another strategy for one player, depending on how the player's opponents may play.

   a. Boolean algebra
   b. Coherence
   c. Concurrent
   d. Dominance

28. In mathematics, the term _____ has several different important meanings:

- An _____ is an equality that remains true regardless of the values of any variables that appear within it, to distinguish it from an equality which is true under more particular conditions. For this, the 'triple bar' symbol ≡ is sometimes used.
- In algebra, an _____ or _____ element of a set S with a binary operation Â· is an element e that, when combined with any element x of S, produces that same x. That is, eÂ·x = xÂ·e = x for all x in S.
    - The _____ function from a set S to itself, often denoted id or id_S, s the function such that i = x for all x in S. This function serves as the _____ element in the set of all functions from S to itself with respect to function composition.
    - In linear algebra, the _____ matrix of size n is the n-by-n square matrix with ones on the main diagonal and zeros elsewhere. This matrix serves as the _____ with respect to matrix multiplication.

A common example of the first meaning is the trigonometric _____

$$\sin^2 \theta + \cos^2 \theta = 1$$

which is true for all real values of θ, as opposed to

$$\cos \theta = 1,$$

which is true only for some values of θ, not all. For example, the latter equation is true when $\theta = 0$, false when $\theta = 2$

The concepts of 'additive _____' and 'multiplicative _____' are central to the Peano axioms. The number 0 is the 'additive _____' for integers, real numbers, and complex numbers. For the real numbers, for all $a \in \mathbb{R}$,

$$0 + a = a,$$

$$a + 0 = a,$$ and

$$0 + 0 = 0.$$

Similarly, The number 1 is the 'multiplicative _____' for integers, real numbers, and complex numbers.

a. Intersection
b. ARIA
c. Identity
d. Action

Chapter 4. Systems of Linear Equations; Matrices 47

29. In linear algebra, the _____ or unit matrix of size n is the n-by-n square matrix with ones on the main diagonal and zeros elsewhere. It is denoted by I_n, or simply by I if the size is immaterial or can be trivially determined by the context. (In some fields, such as quantum mechanics, the _____ is denoted by a boldface one, 1; otherwise it is identical to I.)

   a. Arity
   b. Unital
   c. Identity matrix
   d. Associativity

30. In mathematics, the _____ of a number n is the number that, when added to n, yields zero. The _____ of n is denoted −n. For example, 7 is −7, because 7 + (−7) = 0, and the _____ of −0.3 is 0.3, because −0.3 + 0.3 = 0.

   a. Associativity
   b. Algebraic structure
   c. Arity
   d. Additive inverse

31. In mathematics, a _____ for a number x, denoted by $1/x$ or x^{-1}, is a number which when multiplied by x yields the multiplicative identity, 1. The _____ of x is also called the reciprocal of x. The _____ of a fraction p/q is q/p.

   a. Double exponential
   b. Hyperbolic function
   c. Golden function
   d. Multiplicative inverse

32. In mathematics, the _____s may be described informally in several different ways. The _____s include both rational numbers, such as 42 and −23/129, and irrational numbers, such as pi and the square root of two; or, a _____ can be given by an infinite decimal representation, such as 2.4871773339...., where the digits continue in some way; or, the _____s may be thought of as points on an infinitely long number line.

These descriptions of the _____s, while intuitively accessible, are not sufficiently rigorous for the purposes of pure mathematics.

   a. Minkowski distance
   b. Real number
   c. Pre-algebra
   d. Tally marks

33. In mathematics and in the sciences, a _____ (plural: _____e, formulæ or _____s) is a concise way of expressing information symbolically (as in a mathematical or chemical _____), or a general relationship between quantities. One of many famous _____e is Albert Einstein's $E = mc^2$ (see special relativity

In mathematics, a _____ is a key to solve an equation with variables. For example, the problem of determining the volume of a sphere is one that requires a significant amount of integral calculus to solve.

   a. 120-cell
   b. 1-center problem
   c. 2-3 heap
   d. Formula

34. _____ is the practice and study of hiding information. In modern times, _____ is considered a branch of both mathematics and computer science, and is affiliated closely with information theory, computer security, and engineering. _____ is used in applications present in technologically advanced societies; examples include the security of ATM cards, computer passwords, and electronic commerce, which all depend on _____.
   a. MAGENTA
   b. LOKI
   c. CIKS-1
   d. Cryptography

35. In communication theory and coding theory, _____ is the process of translating received messages into codewords of a given code These methods are often used to recover messages sent over a noisy channel, such as a binary symmetric channel.
   a. Decoding
   b. Fast Folding Algorithm
   c. Hilbert spectrum
   d. MUSHRA

36. In mathematics, and in particular in abstract algebra, distributivity is a property of binary operations that generalises the _____ law from elementary algebra.
   a. Permutation
   b. Distributive
   c. Closure with a twist
   d. General linear group

Chapter 5. Linear Inequalities and Linear Programming

1. _____ is either of the two parts into which a plane divides the three-dimensional space. More generally, a _____ is either of the two parts into which a hyperplane divides an affine space.
   a. Parallelogram law
   b. Half-space
   c. Simple polytope
   d. Pendent

2. In the study of metric spaces in mathematics, there are various notions of two metrics on the same underlying space being 'the same', or _____.

In the following, M will denote a non-empty set and d_1 and d_2 will denote two metrics on M.

The two metrics d_1 and d_2 are said to be topologically _____ if they generate the same topology on M.

   a. A chemical equation
   b. A posteriori
   c. A Mathematical Theory of Communication
   d. Equivalent

3. The mathematical concept of a _____ expresses the intuitive idea of deterministic dependence between two quantities, one of which is viewed as primary and the other as secondary. A _____ then is a way to associate a unique output for each input of a specified type, for example, a real number or an element of a given set.
   a. Going up
   b. Grill
   c. Function
   d. Coherent

4. In mathematics, an _____ is a statement about the relative size or order of two objects, or about whether they are the same or not

   - The notation a < b means that a is less than b.
   - The notation a > b means that a is greater than b.
   - The notation a ≠ b means that a is not equal to b, but does not say that one is bigger than the other or even that they can be compared in size.

In all these cases, a is not equal to b, hence, '_____'.

Chapter 5. Linear Inequalities and Linear Programming

These relations are known as strict _____

- The notation a ≤ b means that a is less than or equal to b;
- The notation a ≥ b means that a is greater than or equal to b;

An additional use of the notation is to show that one quantity is much greater than another, normally by several orders of magnitude.

- The notation a << b means that a is much less than b.
- The notation a >> b means that a is much greater than b.

If the sense of the _____ is the same for all values of the variables for which its members are defined, then the _____ is called an 'absolute' or 'unconditional' _____. If the sense of an _____ holds only for certain values of the variables involved, but is reversed or destroyed for other values of the variables, it is called a conditional _____.

An _____ may appear unsolvable because it only states whether a number is larger or smaller than another number; but it is possible to apply the same operations for equalities to inequalities. For example, to find x for the _____ 10x > 23 one would divide 23 by 10.

a. Inequality
b. A posteriori
c. A Mathematical Theory of Communication
d. A chemical equation

5. In optimization, a candidate solution is a member of a set of possible solutions to a given problem. A candidate solution does not have to be a likely or reasonable solution to the problem. The space of all candidate solutions is called the _____, feasible set, search space, or solution space.

a. Step response
b. Quadratic eigenvalue problem
c. Leapfrog integration
d. Feasible region

6. In mathematics, _____ is a technique for optimization of a linear objective function, subject to linear equality and linear inequality constraints. Informally, _____ determines the way to achieve the best outcome in a given mathematical model given some list of requirements represented as linear equations.

More formally, given a polytope, and a real-valued affine function

$$f(x_1, x_2, \ldots, x_n) = c_1 x_1 + c_2 x_2 + \cdots + c_n x_n + d$$

defined on this polytope, a _____ method will find a point in the polytope where this function has the smallest value.

   a. Linear programming relaxation
   b. Descent direction
   c. Lin-Kernighan
   d. Linear programming

7. A set S of real numbers is called _____ from above if there is a real number k such that k ≥ s for all s in S. The number k is called an upper bound of S. The terms _____ from below and lower bound are similarly defined.
   a. Derivative algebra
   b. Descent
   c. Harmonic series
   d. Bounded

8. A _____ is any physical or virtual entity of limited availability, or anything used to help one earn a living. In most cases, commercial or even ethic factors require _____ allocation through _____ management. Clean drinking water is a _____ required by all people.

As _____ s are very useful, we attach some information value to them.

   a. 1-center problem
   b. 2-3 heap
   c. 120-cell
   d. Resource

9. _____ is an important tool for manufacturing and engineering, where it can have a major impact on the productivity of a process. In manufacturing, the purpose of _____ is to minimize the production time and costs, by telling a production facility what to make, when, with which staff, and on which equipment. Production _____ aims to maximize the efficiency of the operation and reduce costs.

a. Crib
b. Scheduling
c. Boolean algebra
d. Critical point

10. In mathematics, a _____ is a condition that a solution to an optimization problem must satisfy. There are two types of _____s: equality _____s and inequality _____s. The set of solutions that satisfy all _____s is called the feasible set.
   a. Concurrent
   b. Constraint
   c. Decidable
   d. Foci

11. An _____ is a tree data structure in which each internal node has up to eight children. _____s are most often used to partition a three dimensional space by recursively subdividing it into eight octants. _____s are the three-dimensional analog of quadtrees.
   a. Octree
   b. Adaptive k-d tree
   c. Interval tree
   d. External node

12. A _____ is an abstract model that uses mathematical language to describe the behavior of a system. Eykhoff defined a _____ as 'a representation of the essential aspects of an existing system which presents knowledge of that system in usable form'.
   a. Metaheuristic
   b. Rata Die
   c. Total least squares
   d. Mathematical model

13. In mathematics, a _____ is a function whose values do not vary and thus are constant. For example, if we have the function f→ B is a _____ iff f
   a. Squeeze mapping
   b. Point reflection
   c. Linear operator
   d. Constant function

Chapter 5. Linear Inequalities and Linear Programming

14. _____ is an economics theory, that refers to individuals or societies gaining the maximum amount out of the resources they have available to them. The theory proposed by most economists is that _____ refers to the _____ of profit.

As some economists have begun to find out, this theory does not hold true for all people and cultures.

a. Composite
b. Boundary
c. Maximization
d. Homogeneity

15. In mathematics and computer science, an optimization problem is the problem of finding the best solution from all feasible solutions. More formally, an optimization problem A is a quadruple , where

- I is a set of instances;
- given an instance ⬜>, f is the set of feasible solutions;
- given an instance x and a feasible solution y of x, m denotes the measure of y, which is usually a positive real.
- g is the goal function, and is either min or max.

The goal is then to find for some instance x an _____, that is, a feasible solution y with

⬜>

For each optimization problem, there is a corresponding decision problem that asks whether there is a feasible solution for some particular measure m_0. For example, if there is a graph G which contains vertices u and v, an optimization problem might be 'find a path from u to v that uses the fewest edges'. This problem might have an answer of, say, 4.

a. Interactive proof system
b. Approximation algorithms
c. Exponential time
d. Optimal solution

16. In mathematics, an _____ is a theorem with a statement beginning 'there exis ..' y, ... there exis ...'. That is, in more formal terms of symbolic logic, it is a theorem with a statement involving the existential quantifier.

a. A Mathematical Theory of Communication
b. A posteriori
c. A chemical equation
d. Existence theorem

17.   In mathematics, a _____ is a statement that can be proved on the basis of explicitly stated or previously agreed assumptions.
   a. Disjunction introduction
   b. Theorem
   c. Logical value
   d. Boolean function

18.   In chemistry, _____ is the measure of how much of a given substance there is mixed with another substance. This can apply to any sort of chemical mixture, but most frequently the concept is limited to homogeneous solutions, where it refers to the amount of solute in the solvent.

To concentrate a solution, one must add more solute, or reduce the amount of solvent (for instance, by selective evaporation.)

   a. 120-cell
   b. 2-3 heap
   c. 1-center problem
   d. Concentration

19.   In geometry, a _____ or n-_____ is an n-dimensional analogue of a triangle. Specifically, a _____ is the convex hull of a set of affinely independent points in some Euclidean space of dimension n or higher.

For example, a 0-_____ is a point, a 1-_____ is a line segment, a 2-_____ is a triangle, a 3-_____ is a tetrahedron, and a 4-_____ is a pentachoron.

   a. Polytetrahedron
   b. Simplex
   c. Hypercell
   d. Demihypercubes

20.   In mathematical optimization theory, the simplex algorithm, created by the American mathematician George Dantzig in 1947, is a popular algorithm for numerical solution of the linear programming problem. The journal Computing in Science and Engineering listed it as one of the top 10 algorithms of the century.

Chapter 5. Linear Inequalities and Linear Programming

An unrelated, but similarly named method is the Nelder-Mead method or downhill _____ due to Nelder ' Mead and is a numerical method for optimising many-dimensional unconstrained problems, belonging to the more general class of search algorithms.

   a. Differential evolution
   b. Hill climbing
   c. Fibonacci search
   d. Simplex method

21. _____, also sometimes known as standard form or as exponential notation, is a way of writing numbers that accommodates values too large or small to be conveniently written in standard decimal notation. _____ has a number of useful properties and is often favored by scientists, mathematicians and engineers, who work with such numbers.

In _____, numbers are written in the form:

$$a \times 10^b$$

   a. Leading zero
   b. Radix point
   c. Scientific notation
   d. 1-center problem

22. In Linear programming a _____ is a variable which is added to a constraint to turn the inequality into an equation. This is required to turn an inequality into an equality where a linear combination of variables is less than or equal to a given constant in the former. As with the other variables in the augmented constraints, the _____ cannot take on negative values, as the Simplex algorithm requires them to be positive or zero.

   a. Bellman equation
   b. Shape optimization
   c. Shekel function
   d. Slack variable

23. Initial objects are also called _____, and terminal objects are also called final.
   a. Colimit
   b. Terminal object
   c. Direct limit
   d. Coterminal

Chapter 5. Linear Inequalities and Linear Programming

24. In mathematical optimization theory, the _____, created by the North American mathematician George Dantzig in 1947, is a popular technique for numerical solution of the linear programming problem.
    a. Feit–Thompson theorem
    b. Sociable number
    c. Simplex algorithm
    d. Partition

25. In mathematics, an _____ or member of a set is any one of the distinct objects that make up that set.

Writing A = {1,2,3,4}, means that the _____s of the set A are the numbers 1, 2, 3 and 4. Groups of _____s of A, for example {1,2}, are subsets of A.

   a. Ideal
   b. Order
   c. Element
   d. Universal code

26. In the mathematical area of order theory, every partially ordered set P gives rise to a _____ partially ordered set which is often denoted by P^{op} or P^d. This _____ order P^{op} is defined to be the set with the inverse order. It is easy to see that this construction, which can be depicted by flipping the Hasse diagram for P upside down, will indeed yield a partially ordered set.
    a. Dual
    b. Context-sensitive language
    c. Christofides heuristics
    d. Contraction mapping

27. In linear programming, the primary problem and the _____ are complementary. A solution to either one determines a solution to both.

Linear programming problems are optimization problems in which the objective function and the constraints are all linear.

   a. Dual problem
   b. Linear matrix inequality
   c. Topological derivative
   d. Linear programming relaxation

Chapter 5. Linear Inequalities and Linear Programming

28. In mathematics, a _____ is a rectangular table of elements, which may be numbers or, more generally, any abstract quantities that can be added and multiplied. Matrices are used to describe linear equations, keep track of the coefficients of linear transformations and to record data that depend on multiple parameters. Matrices are described by the field of _____ theory.

   a. Coherent
   b. Double counting
   c. Compression
   d. Matrix

29. In mathematics, _____ is the operation of adding two matrices by adding the corresponding entries together. However, there is another operation which could also be considered as a kind of addition for matrices.

The usual _____ is defined for two matrices of the same dimensions.

   a. Standard basis
   b. Spectral theory
   c. Jordan normal form
   d. Matrix addition

30. In linear algebra, the _____ of a matrix A is another matrix A^T created by any one of the following equivalent actions:

   - write the rows of A as the columns of A^T
   - write the columns of A as the rows of A^T
   - reflect A by its main diagonal to obtain A^T

Formally, the _____ of an m × n matrix A is the n × m matrix

$$\mathbf{A}^T_{ij} = \mathbf{A}_{ji} \text{ for } 1 \leq i \leq n, 1 \leq j \leq m.$$

- $\begin{bmatrix} 1 & 2 \\ 3 & 4 \end{bmatrix}^T = \begin{bmatrix} 1 & 3 \\ 2 & 4 \end{bmatrix}.$

- $\begin{bmatrix} 1 & 2 \\ 3 & 4 \\ 5 & 6 \end{bmatrix}^T = \begin{bmatrix} 1 & 3 & 5 \\ 2 & 4 & 6 \end{bmatrix}.$

For matrices A, B and scalar c we have the following properties of _____:

1. $\left(\mathbf{A}^{\mathrm{T}}\right)^{\mathrm{T}} = \mathbf{A}$

    Taking the _____ is an involution.

- $(\mathbf{A} + \mathbf{B})^{\mathrm{T}} = \mathbf{A}^{\mathrm{T}} + \mathbf{B}^{\mathrm{T}}$

    The _____ respects addition.

- $(\mathbf{AB})^{\mathrm{T}} = \mathbf{B}^{\mathrm{T}}\mathbf{A}^{\mathrm{T}}$

    Note that the order of the factors reverses. From this one can deduce that a square matrix A is invertible if and only if A^T is invertible, and in this case we have^T =$^{-1}$. It is relatively easy to extend this result to the general case of multiple matrices, where we find that^T = $Z^T Y^T X^T ... C^T B^T A^T$.

- $(c\mathbf{A})^{\mathrm{T}} = c\mathbf{A}^{\mathrm{T}}$

    The _____ of a scalar is the same scalar. Together with, this states that the _____ is a linear map from the space of m × n matrices to the space of all n × m matrices.

- $\det(\mathbf{A}^{\mathrm{T}}) = \det(\mathbf{A})$

    The determinant of a matrix is the same as that of its _____.

- The dot product of two column vectors a and b can be computed as

    $$\mathbf{a} \cdot \mathbf{b} = \mathbf{a}^{\mathrm{T}}\mathbf{b},$$

which is written as $a_i\, b^i$ in Einstein notation.
- If A has only real entries, then $A^T A$ is a positive-semidefinite matrix.
- $\left(\mathbf{A}^{\mathrm{T}}\right)^{-1} = \left(\mathbf{A}^{-1}\right)^{\mathrm{T}}$

    The _____ of an invertible matrix is also invertible, and its inverse is the _____ of the inverse of the original matrix.

- If A is a square matrix, then its eigenvalues are equal to the eigenvalues of its _____.

A square matrix whose _____ is equal to itself is called a symmetric matrix; that is, A is symmetric if

$$\mathbf{A}^\mathrm{T} = \mathbf{A}.$$

A square matrix whose _____ is also its inverse is called an orthogonal matrix; that is, G is orthogonal if

$$\mathbf{G}\mathbf{G}^\mathrm{T} = \mathbf{G}^\mathrm{T}\mathbf{G} = \mathbf{I}_n,$$ the identity matrix.

A square matrix whose _____ is equal to its negative is called skew-symmetric matrix; that is, A is skew-symmetric if

$$\mathbf{A}^\mathrm{T} = -\mathbf{A}.$$

The conjugate _____ of the complex matrix A, written as A*, is obtained by taking the _____ of A and the complex conjugate of each entry:

$$\mathbf{A}^* = (\overline{\mathbf{A}})^\mathrm{T} = \overline{(\mathbf{A}^\mathrm{T})}.$$

If f: V→W is a linear map between vector spaces V and W with nondegenerate bilinear forms, we define the _____ of f to be the linear map $^t f$: W→V, determined by

$$B_V(v, {}^t f(w)) = B_W(f(v), w) \quad \forall\ v \in V, w \in W.$$

Here, B_V and B_W are the bilinear forms on V and W respectively. The matrix of the _____ of a map is the transposed matrix only if the bases are orthonormal with respect to their bilinear forms.

Over a complex vector space, one often works with sesquilinear forms instead of bilinear.

   a. Polynomial matrix
   b. Tridiagonal matrix
   c. Cartan matrix
   d. Transpose

31. In the geometry of the projective plane, _____ refers to geometric transformations that replace points by lines and lines by points while preserving incidence properties among the transformed objects. The existence of such transformations leads to a general principle, that any theorem about incidences between points and lines in the projective plane may be transformed into another theorem about lines and points, by a substitution of the appropriate words.

_____ in the projective plane is a special case of _____ for projective spaces, transformations that interchange dimension + codimension.

a. Duality
b. Decidable
c. Disk
d. Blocking

32. In Linear programming a _____ is a variable which is subtracted from a constraint to turn the inequality into an equation.

This is required to turn an inequality into an equality where a linear combination of variables is greater than or equal to a given constant in the former. As with the other variables in the augmented constraints, the _____ cannot take on negative values, as the Simplex algorithm requires them to be positive or zero.

a. Successive linear programming
b. Global optimum
c. Quantum annealing
d. Surplus variable

Chapter 6. Logic, Sets, and Counting

1. In logic and mathematics, _____ or not is an operation on logical values, for example, the logical value of a proposition, that sends true to false and false to true. Intuitively, the _____ of a proposition holds exactly when that proposition does not hold. In grammar, nor is an adverb which acts as a coordinating conjunction.
   a. 1-center problem
   b. Negation
   c. Syntax
   d. Sentence diagram

2. In logic and philosophy, _____ refers to either (a) the 'content' or 'meaning' of a meaningful declarative sentence or (b) the pattern of symbols, marks, or sounds that make up a meaningful declarative sentence. _____s in either case are intended to be truth-bearers, that is, they are either true or false.

   The existence of _____s in the former sense, as well as the existence of 'meanings', is disputed.

   a. Proposition
   b. Linear logic
   c. Laws of classical logic
   d. Logicism

3. In logic and mathematics, or, also known as logical _____ or inclusive _____ is a logical operator that results in true whenever one or more of its operands are true. In grammar, or is a coordinating conjunction. In ordinary language 'or' rather has the meaning of exclusive _____.
   a. Zero-point energy
   b. Disjunction
   c. Triquetra
   d. Cube

4. In propositional logic, contraposition is a logical relationship between two statements of material implication. A proposition Q is materially implied by a proposition P when the following relationship holds:

$$(P \to Q)$$

In vernacular terms, this states 'If P then Q', or, 'If Socrates is a man then Socrates is human.' In a conditional such as this, P is called the antecedent and Q the consequent. One statement is the _____ of the other just when its antecedent is the negated consequent of the other, and vice-versa.

Chapter 6. Logic, Sets, and Counting

a. Control chart
b. Continuous signal
c. Contour map
d. Contrapositive

5. A _____ is a mathematical table used in logic -- specifically in connection with Boolean algebra, boolean functions, and propositional calculus -- to compute the functional values of logical expressions on each of their functional arguments, that is, on each combination of values taken by their logical variables. In particular, _____s can be used to tell whether a propositional expression is true for all legitimate input values, that is, logically valid.

The pattern of reasoning that the _____ tabulates was Frege's, Peirce's, and Schröder's by 1880.

a. 1-center problem
b. 2-3 heap
c. Truth table
d. 120-cell

6. In philosophy and logic, _____ is the status of facts that are not logically necessarily true or false.

In philosophy and logic, people draw a distinction between

- possibility: 'If it happened, it must be possible' -- If an event happened, it must be a possible event. A possible statement is not necessarily false. A 'possibility', such as a coincidence, is either a '_____', or a 'necessity' (but not both.)
- _____: a contingent event is an event which 'could have not happened'. Each contingent event is also a possible event, but not vice versa. A contingent statement is not necessarily false, but it is not necessarily true either.
- necessity: a necessary event is an event which 'could not have not happened'. In other words, a necessary event inevitably must have happened. Each necessary event is also a possible event, but not vice versa. A necessary statement is a statement that is necessarily true, such as a tautology.

a. Rigid designator
b. Modal companion
c. Modal operator
d. Contingency

7. In logic and mathematics, _____ is a logical relation that holds between a set T of formulae and a formula B when every model of T is also a model of B. In symbols,

1. $T \models B$
2. $T \Rightarrow B$
3. $T \therefore B$

which may be read 'T implies B, or 'B is a consequence of T'. In such an implication, T is called the antecedent, while B is called the consequent.

In other words, holds when the class of models of T is a subset of the class of models of B.

   a. Logical implication
   b. Thoralf Albert Skolem
   c. Necessary and sufficient
   d. Proposition

8. The function $\log_b(x)$ depends on both b and x, but the term _____ (or logarithmic function) in standard usage refers to a function of the form $\log_b(x)$ in which the base b is fixed and so the only argument is x. Thus there is one _____ for each value of the base b (which must be positive and must differ from 1.) Viewed in this way, the base-b _____ is the inverse function of the exponential function b^x.
   a. Logarithm function
   b. 2-3 heap
   c. 1-center problem
   d. 120-cell

9. _____ In logic, statements p and q are logically equivalent if they have the same logical content.
   a. Realizability
   b. Fallacies of definition
   c. Distribution rule
   d. Logical equivalence

10. The mathematical concept of a _____ expresses the intuitive idea of deterministic dependence between two quantities, one of which is viewed as primary and the other as secondary. A _____ then is a way to associate a unique output for each input of a specified type, for example, a real number or an element of a given set.

Chapter 6. Logic, Sets, and Counting

   a. Going up
   b. Grill
   c. Coherent
   d. Function

11. In mathematics, an _____ or member of a set is any one of the distinct objects that make up that set.

Writing A = {1,2,3,4}, means that the _____s of the set A are the numbers 1, 2, 3 and 4. Groups of _____s of A, for example {1,2}, are subsets of A.

   a. Ideal
   b. Element
   c. Universal code
   d. Order

12. In discrete mathematics and predominantly in set theory, a _____ is a concept used in comparisons of sets to refer to the unique values of one set in relation to another. The terms 'absolute' and 'relative' _____ refer to more specific applications of the concept, with universal _____s referring to elements unique to the universal set and the latter referring to the unique elements of one set in relation to another. In this image, the universal set is represented by the border of the image, and the set A as a disc.
   a. Kernel
   b. Huge
   c. Derivative algebra
   d. Complement

13. In mathematics, and more specifically set theory, the _____ is the unique set having no members. Some axiomatic set theories assure that the _____ exists by including an axiom of _____; in other theories, its existence can be deduced. Many possible properties of sets are trivially true for the _____.
   a. Empty function
   b. A Mathematical Theory of Communication
   c. Inverse function
   d. Empty set

14. In mathematics, a _____ is a set that is negligible in some sense. For different applications, the meaning of 'negligible' varies. In measure theory, any set of measure 0 is called a _____.

Chapter 6. Logic, Sets, and Counting

a. Radonifying function
b. Borel-Cantelli lemma
c. Null set
d. Prevalence and shyness

15. In mathematics, especially in set theory, a set A is a _____ of a set B if A is 'contained' inside B. Notice that A and B may coincide. The relationship of one set being a _____ of another is called inclusion.

a. Horizontal line test
b. Set of all sets
c. Cartesian product
d. Subset

16. In mathematics, the _____ of two sets A and B is the set that contains all elements of A that also belong to B, but no other elements.

For explanation of the symbols used in this article, refer to the table of mathematical symbols.

The _____ of A and B

The _____ of A and B is written 'A ∩ B'. Formally:

x is an element of A ∩ B if and only if
- x is an element of A and
- x is an element of B.

For example:
- The _____ of the sets {1, 2, 3} and {2, 3, 4} is {2, 3}.
- The number 9 is not in the _____ of the set of prime numbers {2, 3, 5, 7, 11, â€¦} and the set of odd numbers {1, 3, 5, 7, 9, 11, â€¦}.

If the _____ of two sets A and B is empty, that is they have no elements in common, then they are said to be disjoint, denoted: A ∩ B = Ø. For example the sets {1, 2} and {3, 4} are disjoint, written
{1, 2} ∩ {3, 4} = Ø.

a. Erlang
b. Advice
c. Order
d. Intersection

Chapter 6. Logic, Sets, and Counting

17. In set theory, the term _____ refers to a set operation used in the convergence of set elements to form a resultant set containing the elements of both sets. As a simple example, a _____ of two disjoint sets, which do not have elements in common results in a set containing all elements from both sets. A Venn diagram representing the _____ of sets A and B.
    a. UES
    b. Introduction
    c. Event
    d. Union

18. _____ or set diagrams are diagrams that show all hypothetically possible logical relations between a finite collection of sets. _____ were invented around 1880 by John Venn. They are used in many fields, including set theory, probability, logic, statistics, and computer science.
    a. 1-center problem
    b. 120-cell
    c. 2-3 heap
    d. Venn diagrams

19. A _____ is a 2D geometric symbolic representation of information according to some visualization technique. Sometimes, the technique uses a 3D visualization which is then projected onto the 2D surface. The word graph is sometimes used as a synonym for _____.
    a. 2-3 heap
    b. 120-cell
    c. 1-center problem
    d. Diagram

20. In mathematics, two sets are said to be disjoint if they have no element in common. For example, {1, 2, 3} and {4, 5, 6} are _____.

Formally, two sets A and B are disjoint if their intersection is the empty set.
wikimedia.org/math/b/3/5/b35d3befc06b831ff4d6cd63bf922efb.png">

This definition extends to any collection of sets.

   a. Horizontal line test
   b. Subset
   c. Preimage
   d. Disjoint sets

21. A _____ is an exclusive group of people who share interests, views, purposes, patterns of behavior, or ethnicity. A _____ as a reference group can be either normative or comparative.

A normative _____ or reference group is often the primary source of social interaction for the members of the _____, which can affect the values and beliefs of an individual.

   a. Clique
   b. 2-3 heap
   c. 1-center problem
   d. 120-cell

22. In mathematics, a _____ is an algebraic structure consisting of a set together with an operation that combines any two of its elements to form a third element. To qualify as a _____, the set and operation must satisfy a few conditions called _____ axioms, namely associativity, identity and invertibility. While these are familiar from many mathematical structures, such as number systems--for example, the integers endowed with the addition operation form a _____--the formulation of the axioms is detached from the concrete nature of the _____ and its operation.
   a. Characteristic function
   b. Derivative algebra
   c. Group
   d. Coherence

23. _____ is the mathematical operation of scaling one number by another. It is one of the four basic operations in elementary arithmetic.

_____ is defined for whole numbers in terms of repeated addition; for example, 4 multiplied by 3 can be calculated by adding 3 copies of 4 together:

$$4 + 4 + 4 = 12.$$

_____ of rational numbers and real numbers is defined by systematic generalization of this basic idea.

   a. Multiplication
   b. Highest common factor
   c. Least common multiple
   d. The number 0 is even.

24. _____ is the process to impart information from a sender to a receiver with the use of a medium. _____ requires that all parties have an area of communicative commonality. There are auditory means, such as speaking, singing and sometimes tone of voice, and nonverbal, physical means, such as body language, sign language, paralanguage, touch, eye contact, or the use of writing.

Chapter 6. Logic, Sets, and Counting

  a. 1-center problem
  b. 2-3 heap
  c. 120-cell
  d. Communication

25. In mathematics, the _____ of a non-negative integer n, denoted by n!, is the product of all positive integers less than or equal to n. For example,

$$5! = 1 \times 2 \times 3 \times 4 \times 5 = 120$$

and
$$6! = 1 \times 2 \times 3 \times 4 \times 5 \times 6 = 720$$

The notation n! was introduced by Christian Kramp in 1808.

The _____ function is formally defined by

$$n! = \prod_{k=1}^{n} k \qquad \forall n \in \mathbb{N}.$$

The above definition incorporates the instance

$$0! = 1$$

as an instance of the fact that the product of no numbers at all is 1.

  a. Partition of a set
  b. Plane partition
  c. Symbolic combinatorics
  d. Factorial

26. In statistics, the _____ problem occurs when one considers a set of statistical inferences simultaneously. Errors in inference, including confidence intervals that fail to include their corresponding population parameters are more likely when one considers the family as a whole.

The term 'comparisons' in _____ typically refers to comparisons of two groups, such as treatment versus control.

Chapter 6. Logic, Sets, and Counting

a. Cross-validation
b. Closed testing procedure
c. Familywise error rate
d. Multiple comparisons

27. _____ consists of 'social relations involving authority or power' and refers to the regulation of a political unit, and to the methods and tactics used to formulate and apply policy.

Political science (also political studies) is the study of political behavior, and examines the acquisition and application of power. Related areas of study include political philosophy, which seeks a rationale for _____ and an ethic of public behavior, and public administration, which examines the practices of governance.

a. 120-cell
b. 2-3 heap
c. 1-center problem
d. Politics

28. In several fields of mathematics the term _____ is used with different but closely related meanings. They all relate to the notion of mapping the elements of a set to other elements of the same set, i.e., exchanging elements of a set.

The general concept of _____ can be defined more formally in different contexts:

In combinatorics, a _____ is usually understood to be a sequence containing each element from a finite set once, and only once.

a. Linearly independent
b. Tensor product
c. Cyclic permutation
d. Permutation

29. In combinatorial mathematics, a _____ is an un-ordered collection of distinct elements, usually of a prescribed size and taken from a given set. Given such a set S, a _____ of elements of S is just a subset of S, where as always forsets the order of the elements is not taken into account. Also, as always forsets, no elements can be repeated more than once in a _____; this is often referred to as a 'collection without repetition'.
a. Heawood number
b. Combination
c. Fill-in
d. Sparsity

Chapter 6. Logic, Sets, and Counting

30. A _____, in mathematics, is a polynomial function of the form $f(x) = ax^2 + bx + c$, where $a \neq 0$. The graph of a _____ is a parabola whose major axis is parallel to the y-axis.

The expression ax² + bx + c in the definition of a _____ is a polynomial of degree 2 or a 2nd degree polynomial, because the highest exponent of x is 2.

   a. Quadratic function
   b. Discriminant
   c. Multivariate division algorithm
   d. Laguerre polynomials

31. In engineering and manufacturing, _____ is involved in developing systems to ensure products or services are designed and produced to meet or exceed customer requirements or SLA's. Genetic algorithms are search techniques, used in computing to find exact or approximate solutions to optimization and search problems.

Alternative _____ procedures can be applied on a process to test statistically the null hypothesis, that the process is in control, against the alternative, that the process is out of control.

   a. 1-center problem
   b. Statistical process control
   c. 120-cell
   d. Quality control

32. An _____ is a decision-making process by which a population chooses an individual to hold formal office. This is the usual mechanism by which modern democracy fills offices in the legislature, sometimes in the executive and judiciary, and for regional and local government. This process is also used in many other private and business organizations, from clubs to voluntary associations and corporations.
   a. Election
   b. A chemical equation
   c. A posteriori
   d. A Mathematical Theory of Communication

33. In mathematics, especially in geometry and group theory, a _____ in R^n is a discrete subgroup of R^n which spans the real vector space R^n. Every _____ in R^n can be generated from a basis for the vector space by forming all linear combinations with integral coefficients. A _____ may be viewed as a regular tiling of a space by a primitive cell.

a. Group
b. Boundary
c. Lattice
d. Homogeneity

Chapter 7. Probability

1. Introduction

In the theory of probability and statistics, a _____ is an experiment whose outcome is random and can be either of two possible outcomes, 'success' and 'failure'.

In practice it refers to a single experiment which can have one of two possible outcomes. These events can be phrased into 'yes or no' questions:

- Did the coin land heads?
- Was the newborn child a girl?
- Were a person's eyes green?
- Did a mosquito die after the area was sprayed with insecticide?
- Did a potential customer decide to buy a product?
- Did a citizen vote for a specific candidate?
- Did an employee vote pro-union?

Therefore success and failure are labels for outcomes, and should not be construed literally. Examples of _____s include

- Flipping a coin. In this context, obverse conventionally denotes success and reverse denotes failure. A fair coin has the probability of success 0.5 by definition.
- Rolling a die, where a six is 'success' and everything else a 'failure'.
- In conducting a political opinion poll, choosing a voter at random to ascertain whether that voter will vote 'yes' in an upcoming referendum.

Mathematically, a _____ can be described by a sample space Ω consisting of two values, s for 'success' and f for 'failure'. Therefore the sample space is $\Omega = \{s, f\}$.

 a. Bernoulli trial
 b. Law of total cumulance
 c. Marginal distribution
 d. Point process

2. In scientific inquiry, an _____ is a method of investigating particular types of research questions or solving particular types of problems. The _____ is a cornerstone in the empirical approach to acquiring deeper knowledge about the world and is used in both natural sciences as well as in social sciences. An _____ is defined, in science, as a method of investigating less known fields, solving practical problems and proving theoretical assumptions.
 a. A posteriori
 b. A chemical equation
 c. A Mathematical Theory of Communication
 d. Experiment

Chapter 7. Probability

3. In probability theory, an _____ is a set of outcomes to which a probability is assigned. Typically, when the sample space is finite, any subset of the sample space is an _____. However, this approach does not work well in cases where the sample space is infinite, most notably when the outcome is a real number.
    a. Equaliser
    b. Information set
    c. Audio compression
    d. Event

4. In statistics, a _____ is a subset of a population. Typically, the population is very large, making a census or a complete enumeration of all the values in the population impractical or impossible. The _____ represents a subset of manageable size.
    a. Duality
    b. Dispersion
    c. Boussinesq approximation
    d. Sample

5. In probability theory, the _____ or universal _____, often denoted S, Ω of an experiment or random trial is the set of all possible outcomes. For example, if the experiment is tossing a coin, the _____ is the set {head, tail}. For tossing a single six-sided die, the _____ is {1, 2, 3, 4, 5, 6}.
    a. Markov chain
    b. Sample space
    c. Marginal distribution
    d. Martingale central limit theorem

6. In abstract algebra, a module S over a ring R is called _____ or irreducible if it is not the zero module 0 and if its only submodules are 0 and S. Understanding the _____ modules over a ring is usually helpful because these modules form the 'building blocks' of all other modules in a certain sense.

Abelian groups are the same as Z-modules.

    a. Harmonic series
    b. Derivation
    c. Basis
    d. Simple

Chapter 7. Probability

7. In game theory, an _____ is a set of moves or strategies taken by the players, or their payoffs resulting from the actions or strategies taken by all players. The two are complementary in that given knowledge of the set of strategies of all players, the final state of the game is known, as are any relevant payoffs. In a game where chance or a random event is involved, the _____ is not known from only the set of strategies, but is only realized when the random even are realized.
   a. Outcome
   b. Algebraic
   c. Autonomous system
   d. Equaliser

8. _____ is the likelihood or chance that something is the case or will happen. Theoretical _____ is used extensively in areas such as statistics, mathematics, science and philosophy to draw conclusions about the likelihood of potential events and the underlying mechanics of complex systems.

The word _____ does not have a consistent direct definition.

   a. Probability
   b. Discrete random variable
   c. Standardized moment
   d. Statistical significance

9. The word _____ denotes information gained by means of observation, experience as opposed to theoretical. A central concept in science and the scientific method is that all evidence must be _____ that is, dependent on evidence or consequences that are observable by the senses. It is usually differentiated from the philosophic usage of empiricism by the use of the adjective '_____' or the adverb 'empirically.' '_____' as an adjective or adverb is used in conjunction with both the natural and social sciences, and refers to the use of working hypotheses that are testable using observation or experiment.
   a. A Mathematical Theory of Communication
   b. A posteriori
   c. Empirical
   d. A chemical equation

10. _____ or experimental probability, is the ratio of the number favorable outcomes to the total number of trials , not in a sample space but in an actual sequence of experiments. In a more general sense, _____ estimates probabilities from experience and observation. The phrase a posteriori probability has also been used an alternative to _____ or relative frequency.

a. A chemical equation
b. A Mathematical Theory of Communication
c. A posteriori
d. Empirical Probability

11. In statistics the _____ of an event i is the number n_i of times the event occurred in the experiment or the study. These frequencies are often graphically represented in histograms.

We speak of absolute frequencies, when the counts n_i themselves are given and of

$$f_i = \frac{n_i}{N} = \frac{n_i}{\sum_i n_i}$$

Taking the f_i for all i and tabulating or plotting them leads to a _____ distribution.

a. Subharmonic
b. Digital room correction
c. Robinson-Dadson curves
d. Frequency

12. The mathematical concept of a _____ expresses the intuitive idea of deterministic dependence between two quantities, one of which is viewed as primary and the other as secondary. A _____ then is a way to associate a unique output for each input of a specified type, for example, a real number or an element of a given set.
a. Coherent
b. Function
c. Grill
d. Going up

13. In geometry, a _____ or n-_____ is an n-dimensional analogue of a triangle. Specifically, a _____ is the convex hull of a set of affinely independent points in some Euclidean space of dimension n or higher.

For example, a 0-_____ is a point, a 1-_____ is a line segment, a 2-_____ is a triangle, a 3-_____ is a tetrahedron, and a 4-_____ is a pentachoron.

a. Demihypercubes
b. Polytetrahedron
c. Hypercell
d. Simplex

14. In mathematical optimization theory, the simplex algorithm, created by the American mathematician George Dantzig in 1947, is a popular algorithm for numerical solution of the linear programming problem. The journal Computing in Science and Engineering listed it as one of the top 10 algorithms of the century.

An unrelated, but similarly named method is the Nelder-Mead method or downhill _____ due to Nelder ' Mead and is a numerical method for optimising many-dimensional unconstrained problems, belonging to the more general class of search algorithms.

a. Fibonacci search
b. Simplex method
c. Differential evolution
d. Hill climbing

15. In mathematics, the _____ of two sets A and B is the set that contains all elements of A that also belong to B, but no other elements.

For explanation of the symbols used in this article, refer to the table of mathematical symbols.

The _____ of A and B

The _____ of A and B is written 'A ∩ B'. Formally:

x is an element of A ∩ B if and only if
- x is an element of A and
- x is an element of B.

For example:
- The _____ of the sets {1, 2, 3} and {2, 3, 4} is {2, 3}.
- The number 9 is not in the _____ of the set of prime numbers {2, 3, 5, 7, 11, â€¦} and the set of odd numbers {1, 3, 5, 7, 9, 11, â€¦}.

If the _____ of two sets A and B is empty, that is they have no elements in common, then they are said to be disjoint, denoted: A ∩ B = ∅. For example the sets {1, 2} and {3, 4} are disjoint, written
{1, 2} ∩ {3, 4} = ∅.

a. Erlang
b. Intersection
c. Advice
d. Order

16. In set theory, the term _____ refers to a set operation used in the convergence of set elements to form a resultant set containing the elements of both sets. As a simple example, a _____ of two disjoint sets, which do not have elements in common results in a set containing all elements from both sets. A Venn diagram representing the _____ of sets A and B.
   a. Introduction
   b. UES
   c. Event
   d. Union

17. In mathematics, two sets are said to be disjoint if they have no element in common. For example, {1, 2, 3} and {4, 5, 6} are _____.

Formally, two sets A and B are disjoint if their intersection is the empty set.
wikimedia.org/math/b/3/5/b35d3befc06b831ff4d6cd63bf922efb.png">

This definition extends to any collection of sets.

   a. Horizontal line test
   b. Preimage
   c. Subset
   d. Disjoint sets

18. In simple terms, two events are _____ if they cannot occur at the same time.

In logic, two _____ propositions are propositions that logically cannot both be true. To say that more than two propositions are _____ may, depending on context mean that no two of them can both be true, or only that they cannot all be true.

   a. Philosophy
   b. Philosophy of mathematics
   c. Determinism
   d. Mutually exclusive

Chapter 7. Probability

19. In discrete mathematics and predominantly in set theory, a _____ is a concept used in comparisons of sets to refer to the unique values of one set in relation to another. The terms 'absolute' and 'relative' _____ refer to more specific applications of the concept, with universal _____s referring to elements unique to the universal set and the latter referring to the unique elements of one set in relation to another. In this image, the universal set is represented by the border of the image, and the set A as a disc.

   a. Complement
   b. Huge
   c. Derivative algebra
   d. Kernel

20. A _____, in mathematics, is a polynomial function of the form $f(x) = ax^2 + bx + c$, where $a \neq 0$. The graph of a _____ is a parabola whose major axis is parallel to the y-axis.

The expression $ax^2 + bx + c$ in the definition of a _____ is a polynomial of degree 2 or a 2nd degree polynomial, because the highest exponent of x is 2.

   a. Multivariate division algorithm
   b. Laguerre polynomials
   c. Quadratic function
   d. Discriminant

21. In engineering and manufacturing, _____ is involved in developing systems to ensure products or services are designed and produced to meet or exceed customer requirements or SLA's. Genetic algorithms are search techniques, used in computing to find exact or approximate solutions to optimization and search problems.

Alternative _____ procedures can be applied on a process to test statistically the null hypothesis, that the process is in control, against the alternative, that the process is out of control.

   a. 1-center problem
   b. Quality control
   c. Statistical process control
   d. 120-cell

22. In probability theory and statistics the _____ in favour of an event or a proposition are the quantity p /, where p is the probability of the event or proposition. The _____ against the same event are / p. For example, if you chose a random day of the week, then the _____ that you would choose a Sunday would be 1/6, not 1/7.

Chapter 7. Probability

a. Anscombe transform
b. Odds
c. Estimation of covariance matrices
d. Event

23. The _____ is a lay term used to express a belief that outcomes of a random event shall 'even out' within a small sample.

As invoked in everyday life, the 'law' usually reflects bad statistics or wishful thinking rather than any mathematical principle. While there is a real theorem that a random variable will reflect its underlying probability over a very large sample, the _____ typically assumes that unnatural short-term 'balance' must occur.

a. Law of averages
b. 2-3 heap
c. 1-center problem
d. 120-cell

24. The _____ is a theorem in probability that describes the long-term stability of the mean of a random variable. Given a random variable with a finite expected value, if its values are repeatedly sampled, as the number of these observations increases, their mean will tend to approach and stay close to the expected value.

The LLN can easily be illustrated using the rolls of a die.

a. Point process
b. Graphical model
c. Random field
d. Law of large numbers

25. A _____ is the result of applying a function to a set of data.

More formally, statistical theory defines a _____ as a function of a sample where the function itself is independent of the sample's distribution: the term is used both for the function and for the value of the function on a given sample.

A _____ is distinct from an unknown statistical parameter, which is not computable from a sample.

a. Parameter space
b. Spatial dependence
c. Loss function
d. Statistic

26. _____ is a mathematical science pertaining to the collection, analysis, interpretation or explanation, and presentation of data. It also provides tools for prediction and forecasting based on data. It is applicable to a wide variety of academic disciplines, from the natural and social sciences to the humanities, government and business.
    a. Percentile rank
    b. Probability distribution
    c. Regression toward the mean
    d. Statistics

27. In mathematics, an _____, or central tendency of a data set refers to a measure of the 'middle' or 'expected' value of the data set. There are many different descriptive statistics that can be chosen as a measurement of the central tendency of the data items.

An _____ is a single value that is meant to typify a list of values.

   a. A chemical equation
   b. A posteriori
   c. A Mathematical Theory of Communication
   d. Average

28. A _____ is a structured activity, usually undertaken for enjoyment and sometimes also used as an educational tool. _____s are distinct from work, which is usually carried out for remuneration, and from art, which is more concerned with the expression of ideas. However, the distinction is not clear-cut, and many _____s are also considered to be work (such as professional players of spectator sports/_____s) or art (such as jigsaw puzzles or _____s involving an artistic layout such as Mah-jongg solitaire.)
    a. Game
    b. 120-cell
    c. 2-3 heap
    d. 1-center problem

Chapter 7. Probability 81

29. In mathematics and physics, there are a _____ number of topics named in honor of Leonhard Euler. As well, many of these topics include their own unique function, equation, formula, identity, number, or other mathematical entity. Unfortunately however, many of these entities have been given simple names like Euler's function, Euler's equation, and Euler's formula, which are further confused by variations of the 'Euler'-prefix Overall though, Euler's work touched upon so many fields that he is often the earliest written reference on a given matter.

   a. List of trigonometry topics
   b. List of integrals of logarithmic functions
   c. List of mathematical knots and links
   d. Large

30. _____ is the probability of some event A, given the occurrence of some other event B. _____ is written P[A|B], and is read 'the probability of A, given B'.

Joint probability is the probability of two events in conjunction. That is, it is the probability of both events together. The joint probability of A and B is written $P(A \cap B)$ or $P(A,B)$.

   a. Quantile
   b. Renewal theory
   c. Sample space
   d. Conditional probability

31. _____ consists of 'social relations involving authority or power' and refers to the regulation of a political unit, and to the methods and tactics used to formulate and apply policy.

Political science (also political studies) is the study of political behavior, and examines the acquisition and application of power. Related areas of study include political philosophy, which seeks a rationale for _____ and an ethic of public behavior, and public administration, which examines the practices of governance.

   a. 1-center problem
   b. 120-cell
   c. Politics
   d. 2-3 heap

32. The _____ governs the differentiation of products of differentiable functions.
   a. Product rule
   b. 120-cell
   c. Reciprocal Rule
   d. 1-center problem

Chapter 7. Probability

33. In set theory, a _____ is a partially ordered set such that for each t ∈ T, the set {s ∈ T : s < t} is well-ordered by the relation <. For each t ∈ T, the order type of {s ∈ T : s < t} is called the height of t. The height of T itself is the least ordinal greater than the height of each element of T.
    a. Definable numbers
    b. Set-theoretic topology
    c. Tree
    d. Transitive reduction

34. A _____ is a 2D geometric symbolic representation of information according to some visualization technique. Sometimes, the technique uses a 3D visualization which is then projected onto the 2D surface. The word graph is sometimes used as a synonym for _____.
    a. 120-cell
    b. Diagram
    c. 2-3 heap
    d. 1-center problem

35. A _____ is the counterpart to a deterministic process in probability theory. Instead of dealing with only one possible 'reality' of how the process might evolve under time, in a stochastic or random process there is some indeterminacy in its future evolution described by probability distributions. This means that even if the initial condition is known, there are many possibilities the process might go to, but some paths are more probable and others less.
    a. Fractional Brownian motion
    b. Stochastic simulation
    c. Mixing time
    d. Stochastic process

36. _____ , a discipline of biology, is the science of heredity and variation in living organisms. The fact that living things inherit traits from their parents has been used since prehistoric times to improve crop plants and animals through selective breeding. However, the modern science of _____, which seeks to understand the process of inheritance, only began with the work of Gregor Mendel in the mid-nineteenth century.
    a. Hardy-Weinberg principle
    b. Polytomy
    c. Fitness landscapes
    d. Genetics

37. A _____, from the French patron, is a type of theme of recurring events of or objects, sometimes referred to as elements of a set. These elements repeat in a predictable manner. It can be a template or model which can be used to generate things or parts of a thing, especially if the things that are created have enough in common for the underlying _____ to be inferred, in which case the things are said to exhibit the unique _____.

a. 2-3 heap
b. 1-center problem
c. 120-cell
d. Pattern

38. In statistics, the terms Type I error and type II error are used to describe possible errors made in a statistical decision process. In 1928, Jerzy Neyman and Egon Pearson, both eminent statisticians, discussed the problems associated with 'deciding whether or not a particular sample may be judged as likely to have been randomly drawn from a certain population': and identified 'two sources of error', namely:

   null hypothesis, and
   null hypothesis

In 1930, they elaborated on these two sources of error, remarking that 'in testing hypotheses two considerations must be kept in view, we must be able to reduce the chance of rejecting a true hypothesis to as low a value as desired; the test must be so devised that it will reject the hypothesis tested when it is likely to be false'

When an observer makes a Type I error in evaluating a sample against its parent population, s/he is mistakenly thinking that a statistical difference exists when in truth there is no statistical difference. For example, imagine that a pregnancy test has produced a 'positive' result; if the woman is actually not pregnant though, then we say the test produced a '_____'.

a. Mathematical statistics
b. Covariance
c. False positive
d. Chi-square test

39. In mathematics and in the sciences, a _____ (plural: _____e, formulæ or _____s) is a concise way of expressing information symbolically (as in a mathematical or chemical _____), or a general relationship between quantities. One of many famous _____e is Albert Einstein's E = mc² (see special relativity

In mathematics, a _____ is a key to solve an equation with variables. For example, the problem of determining the volume of a sphere is one that requires a significant amount of integral calculus to solve.

a. Formula
b. 1-center problem
c. 2-3 heap
d. 120-cell

Chapter 7. Probability

40. In statistics, a _____ is a graphical display of tabulated frequencies, shown as bars. It shows what proportion of cases fall into each of several categories. A _____ differs from a bar chart in that it is the area of the bar that denotes the value, not the height as in bar charts, a crucial distinction when the categories are not of uniform width.
   a. First-hitting-time models
   b. Histogram
   c. Standardized moment
   d. Probability distribution

41. In differential geometry, a discipline within mathematics, a _____ is a subset of the tangent bundle of a manifold satisfying certain properties. _____s are used to build up notions of integrability, and specifically of a foliation of a manifold
   a. Discontinuity
   b. Distribution
   c. Constraint
   d. Coherence

42. In probability theory and statistics, a _____ identifies either the probability of each value of an unidentified random variable, or the probability of the value falling within a particular interval. The probability function describes the range of possible values that a random variable can attain and the probability that the value of the random variable is within any subset of that range.

When the random variable takes values in the set of real numbers, the _____ is completely described by the cumulative distribution function, whose value at each real x is the probability that the random variable is smaller than or equal to x.

   a. Z-test
   b. Statistical graphics
   c. Normal distribution
   d. Probability distribution

43. In mathematics, _____ are used in the study of chance and probability. They were developed to assist in the analysis of games of chance, stochastic events, and the results of scientific experiments by capturing only the mathematical properties necessary to answer probabilistic questions. Further formalizations have firmly grounded the entity in the theoretical domains of mathematics by making use of measure theory.
   a. Statistics
   b. Median polish
   c. Random variables
   d. Statistical dispersion

Chapter 7. Probability

44. In probability theory and statistics, the _____ of a random variable is the integral of the random variable with respect to its probability measure. For discrete random variables this is equivalent to the probability-weighted sum of the possible values, and for continuous random variables with a density function it is the probability density -weighted integral of the possible values.

The _____ may be intuitively understood by the law of large numbers: The _____, when it exists, is almost surely the limit of the sample mean as sample size grows to infinity.

 a. Expected value
 b. Event
 c. Infinitely divisible distribution
 d. Illustration

45. _____ is the discipline comprising the philosophy, theory, methodology, and professional practice necessary to address important decisions in a formal manner. _____ includes many procedures, methods, and tools for identifying, clearly representing, and formally assessing the important aspects of a decision situation, for prescribing the recommended course of action by applying the maximum expected utility action axiom to a well-formed representation of the decision, and for translating the formal representation of a decision and its corresponding recommendation into insight for the decision maker and other stakeholders.

The term _____ was coined in 1964 by Ronald A.

 a. Gittins index
 b. Decision analysis
 c. Seven Management and Planning Tools
 d. Choice

46. A _____ is a form of gambling which involves the drawing of lots for a prize. Some governments outlaw it, while others endorse it to the extent of organizing a national _____. It is common to find some degree of regulation of _____ by governments.
 a. 1-center problem
 b. Lottery
 c. 2-3 heap
 d. 120-cell

Chapter 8. Data Description and Probability Distributions

1. A bar chart or _____ is a chart with rectangular bars with lengths proportional to the values that they represent. Bar charts are used for comparing two or more values. The bars can be horizontally or vertically oriented.
   a. 120-cell
   b. 1-center problem
   c. 2-3 heap
   d. Bar graph

2. In mathematics, the concept of a _____ tries to capture the intuitive idea of a geometrical one-dimensional and continuous object. A simple example is the circle. In everyday use of the term '_____', a straight line is not curved, but in mathematical parlance _____s include straight lines and line segments.
   a. Kappa curve
   b. Quadrifolium
   c. Curve
   d. Negative pedal curve

3. _____ is finding a curve which has the best fit to a series of data points and possibly other constraints. This section is an introduction to both interpolation and regression analysis. Both are sometimes used for extrapolation.
   a. Numerical stability
   b. Spectral methods
   c. Curve fitting
   d. Multiphysics

4. _____ is that which is owed; usually referencing assets owed, but the term can cover other obligations. In the case of assets, _____ is a means of using future purchasing power in the present before a summation has been earned.
   a. Cobb-Douglas
   b. Point-slope form
   c. Metaheuristic
   d. Debt

5. _____: A graph using line segments to join the plotted points to represent data over time.
   a. Closed under some operation
   b. Broken-line graph
   c. Conditional factor demand
   d. Control theory

Chapter 8. Data Description and Probability Distributions

6. _____ is the change in population over time, and can be quantified as the change in the number of individuals in a population using 'per unit time' for measurement. The term _____ can technically refer to any species, but almost always refers to humans, and it is often used informally for the more specific demographic term _____ rate, and is often used to refer specifically to the growth of the population of the world.

Simple models of _____ include the Malthusian Growth Model and the logistic model.

   a. 1-center problem
   b. 120-cell
   c. Population dynamics
   d. Population growth

7. In signal processing, the _____ E_s of a continuous-time signal x

$$E_s = \langle x(t), x(t) \rangle = \int_{-\infty}^{\infty} |x(t)|^2 dt$$

_____ in this context is not, strictly speaking, the same as the conventional notion of _____ in physics and the other sciences. The two concepts are, however, closely related, and it is possible to convert from one to the other:

$$E = \frac{E_s}{Z} = \frac{1}{Z} \int_{-\infty}^{\infty} |x(t)|^2 dt$$

where Z represents the magnitude, in appropriate units of measure, of the load driven by the signal.

For example, if x

   a. Energy
   b. Audio signal processing
   c. Essential bandwidth
   d. Emphasis

8. In set theory and its applications throughout mathematics, a _____ is a collection of sets that can be unambiguously defined by a property that all its members share. The precise definition of '_____' depends on foundational context. In work on ZF set theory, the notion of _____ is informal, whereas other set theories, such as NBG set theory, axiomatize the notion of '_____'.

a. Congruent
b. Class
c. Coherence
d. Filter

9. In statistics the _____ of an event i is the number n_i of times the event occurred in the experiment or the study. These frequencies are often graphically represented in histograms.

We speak of absolute frequencies, when the counts n_i themselves are given and of

$$f_i = \frac{n_i}{N} = \frac{n_i}{\sum_i n_i}$$

Taking the f_i for all i and tabulating or plotting them leads to a _____ distribution.

a. Digital room correction
b. Frequency
c. Robinson-Dadson curves
d. Subharmonic

10. In mathematics, a _____ is a set of real numbers with the property that any number that lies between two numbers in the set is also included in the set. For example, the set of all numbers x satisfying $0 \leq x \leq 1$ is an _____ which contains 0 and 1, as well as all numbers between them. Other examples of _____s are the set of all real numbers $\mathbb{R}$, the set of all positive real numbers, and the empty set.

a. Annihilator
b. Order
c. Ideal
d. Interval

11. In descriptive statistics, the _____ is the length of the smallest interval which contains all the data. It is calculated by subtracting the smallest observations from the greatest and provides an indication of statistical dispersion.

It is measured in the same units as the data.

a. Class
b. Range
c. Kernel
d. Bandwidth

12. Introduction

In the theory of probability and statistics, a _____ is an experiment whose outcome is random and can be either of two possible outcomes, 'success' and 'failure'.

In practice it refers to a single experiment which can have one of two possible outcomes. These events can be phrased into 'yes or no' questions:

- Did the coin land heads?
- Was the newborn child a girl?
- Were a person's eyes green?
- Did a mosquito die after the area was sprayed with insecticide?
- Did a potential customer decide to buy a product?
- Did a citizen vote for a specific candidate?
- Did an employee vote pro-union?

Therefore success and failure are labels for outcomes, and should not be construed literally. Examples of _____s include

- Flipping a coin. In this context, obverse conventionally denotes success and reverse denotes failure. A fair coin has the probability of success 0.5 by definition.
- Rolling a die, where a six is 'success' and everything else a 'failure'.
- In conducting a political opinion poll, choosing a voter at random to ascertain whether that voter will vote 'yes' in an upcoming referendum.

Mathematically, a _____ can be described by a sample space Ω consisting of two values, s for 'success' and f for 'failure'. Therefore the sample space is $\Omega = \{s, f\}$.

a. Point process
b. Marginal distribution
c. Law of total cumulance
d. Bernoulli trial

13. In statistics, a _____ is a list of the values that a variable takes in a sample. It is usually a list, ordered by quantity, showing the number of times each value appears. For example, if 100 people rate a five-point Likert scale assessing their agreement with a statement on a scale on which 1 denotes strong agreement and 5 strong disagreement, the _____ of their responses might look like:

This simple tabulation has two drawbacks.

- a. Percentile
- b. Confounding
- c. Covariance
- d. Frequency distribution

14. In differential geometry, a discipline within mathematics, a _____ is a subset of the tangent bundle of a manifold satisfying certain properties. _____s are used to build up notions of integrability, and specifically of a foliation of a manifold
- a. Discontinuity
- b. Coherence
- c. Constraint
- d. Distribution

15. _____ is the likelihood or chance that something is the case or will happen. Theoretical _____ is used extensively in areas such as statistics, mathematics, science and philosophy to draw conclusions about the likelihood of potential events and the underlying mechanics of complex systems.

The word _____ does not have a consistent direct definition.

- a. Statistical significance
- b. Probability
- c. Standardized moment
- d. Discrete random variable

16. In probability theory and statistics, a _____ identifies either the probability of each value of an unidentified random variable, or the probability of the value falling within a particular interval. The probability function describes the range of possible values that a random variable can attain and the probability that the value of the random variable is within any subset of that range.

When the random variable takes values in the set of real numbers, the _____ is completely described by the cumulative distribution function, whose value at each real x is the probability that the random variable is smaller than or equal to x.

Chapter 8. Data Description and Probability Distributions

a. Probability distribution
b. Statistical graphics
c. Normal distribution
d. Z-test

17. In statistics, a _____ is a graphical display of tabulated frequencies, shown as bars. It shows what proportion of cases fall into each of several categories. A _____ differs from a bar chart in that it is the area of the bar that denotes the value, not the height as in bar charts, a crucial distinction when the categories are not of uniform width.
    a. Standardized moment
    b. Histogram
    c. First-hitting-time models
    d. Probability distribution

18. In geometry a _____ is traditionally a plane figure that is bounded by a closed path or circuit, composed of a finite sequence of straight line segments. These segments are called its edges or sides, and the points where two edges meet are the _____'s vertices or corners. The interior of the _____ is sometimes called its body.
    a. Regular polygon
    b. Polygonal curve
    c. Parallelogon
    d. Polygon

19. An _____ is a curved shape, figure, or feature. A secant _____ of sharpness E = 120 / 100 = 1.2

In ballistics or aerodynamics, an _____ is a pointed, curved surface mainly used to form the approximately streamlined nose of a bullet, shell, missile or aircraft.

The traditional or secant _____ is a surface of revolution of the same curve that forms a Gothic arch; that is, a circular arc, of greater radius than the diameter of the cylindrical section, is drawn from the edge of the shank until it intercepts the axis.

   a. Oval
   b. Ogive
   c. Epispiral
   d. Isochrone

20. In set theory, a _____ is a small model of Zermelo-Fraenkel set theory with desirable properties. The exact definition depends on the context. In most cases, there is a technical definition of 'premouse' and an added condition of iterability: a _____ is then an iterable premouse.

a. Logical graph
b. Shelah cardinal
c. Maximal consistent set
d. Mouse

21. In computational complexity theory, an algorithm is said to take _____ if the asymptotic upper bound for the time it requires is proportional to the size of the input, which is usually denoted n.

Informally spoken, the running time increases linearly with the size of the input. For example, a procedure that adds up all elements of a list requires time proportional to the length of the list.

a. Truth table reduction
b. Constructible function
c. Time-constructible function
d. Linear time

22. In the physical sciences, _____ is a measurement of the gravitational force acting on an object. Near the surface of the Earth, the acceleration due to gravity is approximately constant; this means that an object's _____ is roughly proportional to its mass.

In commerce and in many other applications, _____ means the same as mass as that term is used in physics.

a. 1-center problem
b. Weight
c. 120-cell
d. 2-3 heap

23. In geometry, a _____ of a triangle is a line segment joining a vertex to the midpoint of the opposing side. Every triangle has exactly three _____s; one running from each vertex to the opposite side.

The three _____s are concurrent at a point known as the triangle's centroid, or center of mass of the triangle.

a. Percentile rank
b. Statistical significance
c. Correlation
d. Median

Chapter 8. Data Description and Probability Distributions

24. In statistics, _____ has two related meanings:

    - the arithmetic _____.
    - the expected value of a random variable, which is also called the population _____.

It is sometimes stated that the '_____' _____s average. This is incorrect if '_____' is taken in the specific sense of 'arithmetic _____' as there are different types of averages: the _____, median, and mode. For instance, average house prices almost always use the median value for the average.

For a real-valued random variable X, the _____ is the expectation of X.

   a. Proportional hazards model
   b. Mean
   c. Statistical population
   d. Probability

25. In mathematics the concept of a _____ generalizes notions such as 'length', 'area', and 'volume'. Informally, given some base set, a '_____' is any consistent assignment of 'sizes' to the subsets of the base set. Depending on the application, the 'size' of a subset may be interpreted as its physical size, the amount of something that lies within the subset, or the probability that some random process will yield a result within the subset.
   a. Lattice
   b. Congruent
   c. Cusp
   d. Measure

26. In mathematics, an _____, or central tendency of a data set refers to a measure of the 'middle' or 'expected' value of the data set. There are many different descriptive statistics that can be chosen as a measurement of the central tendency of the data items.

An _____ is a single value that is meant to typify a list of values.

   a. A Mathematical Theory of Communication
   b. A chemical equation
   c. A posteriori
   d. Average

27. In mathematics, an average, or _____ of a data set refers to a measure of the 'middle' or 'expected' value of the data set. There are many different descriptive statistics that can be chosen as a measurement of the _____ of the data items.

An average is a single value that is meant to typify a list of values.

a. Central tendency
b. Mean reciprocal rank
c. Quartile
d. Trimean

28. In optics, _____ is the phenomenon in which the phase velocity of a wave depends on its frequency. Media having such a property are termed dispersive media.

The most familiar example of _____ is probably a rainbow, in which _____ causes the spatial separation of a white light into components of different wavelengths.

a. Crib
b. Boussinesq approximation
c. Depth
d. Dispersion

29. _____ is the addition of a set of numbers; the result is their sum or total. An interim or present total of a _____ process is termed the running total. The 'numbers' to be summed may be natural numbers, complex numbers, matrices, or still more complicated objects.
a. Summation
b. 120-cell
c. 1-center problem
d. 2-3 heap

30. In statistics, a _____ is a subset of a population. Typically, the population is very large, making a census or a complete enumeration of all the values in the population impractical or impossible. The _____ represents a subset of manageable size.
a. Dispersion
b. Boussinesq approximation
c. Duality
d. Sample

31. _____ and sample covariance are statistics computed from a collection of data, thought of as being random.

Given a random sample $\mathbf{x}_1, \ldots, \mathbf{x}_N$ from an n-dimensional random variable $\mathbf{X}$, the _____ is

$$\bar{\mathbf{x}} = \frac{1}{N} \sum_{k=1}^{N} \mathbf{x}_k.$$

In coordinates, writing the vectors as columns,

$$\mathbf{x}_k = \begin{bmatrix} x_{1k} \\ \vdots \\ x_{nk} \end{bmatrix}, \quad \bar{\mathbf{x}} = \begin{bmatrix} \bar{x}_1 \\ \vdots \\ \bar{x}_n \end{bmatrix},$$

the entries of the _____ are

$$\bar{x}_i = \frac{1}{N} \sum_{k=1}^{N} x_{ik}, \quad i = 1, \ldots, n.$$

The sample covariance of $\mathbf{x}_1, \ldots, \mathbf{x}_N$ is the n-by-n matrix $\mathbf{Q} = [q_{ij}]$ with the entries given by

$$q_{ij} = \frac{1}{N-1} \sum_{k=1}^{N} (x_{ik} - \bar{x}_i)(x_{jk} - \bar{x}_j)$$

The _____ and the sample covariance matrix are unbiased estimates of the mean and the covariance matrix of the random variable $\mathbf{X}$. The reason why the sample covariance matrix has $N-1$ in the denominator rather than N is essentially that the population mean E is not known and is replaced by the _____ $\bar{x}$.

    a. Skewness
    b. Mathematical statistics
    c. Covariance
    d. Sample Mean

32. In statistics, the _____ is the value that occurs the most frequently in a data set or a probability distribution. In some fields, notably education, sample data are often called scores, and the sample _____ is known as the modal score.

Like the statistical mean and the median, the _____ is a way of capturing important information about a random variable or a population in a single quantity.

a. Mode
b. Deltoid
c. Field
d. Function

33. Given an assembly of elements, the number of which decreases ultimately to zero, the _____ is a certain number that characterizes the rate of reduction of the assembly. Specifically, if the individual _____ of an element of the assembly is the time elapsed between some reference time and the removal of that element from the assembly, the mean _____ is the arithmetic mean of the individual _____s.

Typically, the notion of mean _____ is used in connection with exponential decay.

a. Battle of the Sexes
b. Bertrand paradox
c. Going up
d. Lifetime

34. In statistics, the _____ or _____ function is the partial derivative, with respect to some parameter θ, of the logarithm of the likelihood function. If the observation is X and its likelihood is L, then the _____ V can be found through the chain rule:

$$V = \frac{\partial}{\partial \theta} \log L(\theta; X) = \frac{1}{L(\theta; X)} \frac{\partial L(\theta; X)}{\partial \theta}.$$

Note that V is a function of θ and the observation X, so that, in general, it is not a statistic. Note also that V indicates the sensitivity of L.

a. Cleaver
b. Score
c. Functional
d. Deviation

35. In mathematics and statistics, _____ is a measure of difference for interval and ratio variables between the observed value and the mean. The sign of _____, either positive or negative, indicates whether the observation is larger than or smaller than the mean. The magnitude of the value reports how different an observation is from the mean.

a. Filter
b. Functional
c. Conchoid
d. Deviation

36. In probability theory and statistics, the _____ of a random variable, probability distribution averaging the squared distance of its possible values from the expected value. Whereas the mean is a way to describe the location of a distribution, the _____ is a way to capture its scale or degree of being spread out. The unit of _____ is the square of the unit of the original variable.
   a. Nonlinear regression
   b. Probability distribution
   c. Variance
   d. Kendall tau rank correlation coefficient

37. In probability and statistics, the _____ is a measure of the dispersion of a collection of numbers. It can apply to a probability distribution, a random variable, a population or a data set. The _____ is usually denoted with the letter σ.
   a. Statistical population
   b. Failure rate
   c. Null hypothesis
   d. Standard deviation

38. The _____ is a theorem in probability that describes the long-term stability of the mean of a random variable. Given a random variable with a finite expected value, if its values are repeatedly sampled, as the number of these observations increases, their mean will tend to approach and stay close to the expected value.

The LLN can easily be illustrated using the rolls of a die.

   a. Random field
   b. Point process
   c. Law of large numbers
   d. Graphical model

39. A _____ is the result of applying a function to a set of data.

More formally, statistical theory defines a _____ as a function of a sample where the function itself is independent of the sample's distribution: the term is used both for the function and for the value of the function on a given sample.

Chapter 8. Data Description and Probability Distributions

A _____ is distinct from an unknown statistical parameter, which is not computable from a sample.

a. Statistic
b. Parameter space
c. Spatial dependence
d. Loss function

40. _____ is a mathematical science pertaining to the collection, analysis, interpretation or explanation, and presentation of data. It also provides tools for prediction and forecasting based on data. It is applicable to a wide variety of academic disciplines, from the natural and social sciences to the humanities, government and business.

a. Regression toward the mean
b. Probability distribution
c. Percentile rank
d. Statistics

41. In mathematics and physics, there are a _____ number of topics named in honor of Leonhard Euler . As well, many of these topics include their own unique function, equation, formula, identity, number, or other mathematical entity. Unfortunately however, many of these entities have been given simple names like Euler's function, Euler's equation, and Euler's formula, which are further confused by variations of the 'Euler'-prefix Overall though, Euler's work touched upon so many fields that he is often the earliest written reference on a given matter.

a. List of trigonometry topics
b. List of integrals of logarithmic functions
c. List of mathematical knots and links
d. Large

42. The _____ is a lay term used to express a belief that outcomes of a random event shall 'even out' within a small sample.

As invoked in everyday life, the 'law' usually reflects bad statistics or wishful thinking rather than any mathematical principle. While there is a real theorem that a random variable will reflect its underlying probability over a very large sample, the _____ typically assumes that unnatural short-term 'balance' must occur.

a. 2-3 heap
b. 120-cell
c. 1-center problem
d. Law of averages

Chapter 8. Data Description and Probability Distributions

43. A _____, in mathematics, is a polynomial function of the form $f(x) = ax^2 + bx + c$, where $a \neq 0$. The graph of a _____ is a parabola whose major axis is parallel to the y-axis.

The expression ax² + bx + c in the definition of a _____ is a polynomial of degree 2 or a 2nd degree polynomial, because the highest exponent of x is 2.

   a. Multivariate division algorithm
   b. Laguerre polynomials
   c. Discriminant
   d. Quadratic function

44. In engineering and manufacturing, _____ is involved in developing systems to ensure products or services are designed and produced to meet or exceed customer requirements or SLA's. Genetic algorithms are search techniques, used in computing to find exact or approximate solutions to optimization and search problems.

Alternative _____ procedures can be applied on a process to test statistically the null hypothesis, that the process is in control, against the alternative, that the process is out of control.

   a. 120-cell
   b. Statistical process control
   c. 1-center problem
   d. Quality control

45. The mathematical concept of a _____ expresses the intuitive idea of deterministic dependence between two quantities, one of which is viewed as primary and the other as secondary. A _____ then is a way to associate a unique output for each input of a specified type, for example, a real number or an element of a given set.
   a. Coherent
   b. Grill
   c. Going up
   d. Function

46. In elementary algebra, a _____ is a polynomial with two terms: the sum of two monomials. It is the simplest kind of polynomial except for a monomial.

The _____ a² - b² can be factored as the product of two other _____s:

   a² - b² .

The product of a pair of linear _____s a x + b and c x + d is:

2 +x + bd.

A _____ raised to the nth power, represented as

n

can be expanded by means of the _____ theorem or, equivalently, using Pascal's triangle.

a. Rational root theorem
b. Cylindrical algebraic decomposition
c. Real structure
d. Binomial

47.   In scientific inquiry, an _____ is a method of investigating particular types of research questions or solving particular types of problems. The _____ is a cornerstone in the empirical approach to acquiring deeper knowledge about the world and is used in both natural sciences as well as in social sciences. An _____ is defined, in science, as a method of investigating less known fields, solving practical problems and proving theoretical assumptions.
a. A posteriori
b. A Mathematical Theory of Communication
c. A chemical equation
d. Experiment

48.   In mathematics and in the sciences, a _____ (plural: _____e, formulæ or _____s) is a concise way of expressing information symbolically (as in a mathematical or chemical _____), or a general relationship between quantities. One of many famous _____e is Albert Einstein's E = mc^2 (see special relativity

In mathematics, a _____ is a key to solve an equation with variables. For example, the problem of determining the volume of a sphere is one that requires a significant amount of integral calculus to solve.

a. 1-center problem
b. 120-cell
c. Formula
d. 2-3 heap

Chapter 8. Data Description and Probability Distributions

49. In probability theory and statistics, the _____ is the discrete probability distribution of the number of successes in a sequence of n independent yes/no experiments, each of which yields success with probability p. Such a success/failure experiment is also called a Bernoulli experiment or Bernoulli trial. In fact, when n = 1, the _____ is a Bernoulli distribution.
   a. Binomial distribution
   b. Biostatistics
   c. Coefficient of variation
   d. Median

50. In mathematics, _____ are used in the study of chance and probability. They were developed to assist in the analysis of games of chance, stochastic events, and the results of scientific experiments by capturing only the mathematical properties necessary to answer probabilistic questions. Further formalizations have firmly grounded the entity in the theoretical domains of mathematics by making use of measure theory.
   a. Statistics
   b. Median polish
   c. Random variables
   d. Statistical dispersion

51. In probability theory and statistics, the _____ of a random variable is the integral of the random variable with respect to its probability measure. For discrete random variables this is equivalent to the probability-weighted sum of the possible values, and for continuous random variables with a density function it is the probability density-weighted integral of the possible values.

The _____ may be intuitively understood by the law of large numbers: The _____, when it exists, is almost surely the limit of the sample mean as sample size grows to infinity.

   a. Illustration
   b. Expected value
   c. Event
   d. Infinitely divisible distribution

52. _____ , a discipline of biology, is the science of heredity and variation in living organisms. The fact that living things inherit traits from their parents has been used since prehistoric times to improve crop plants and animals through selective breeding. However, the modern science of _____, which seeks to understand the process of inheritance, only began with the work of Gregor Mendel in the mid-nineteenth century.

a. Hardy-Weinberg principle
b. Fitness landscapes
c. Polytomy
d. Genetics

53. In mathematics, specifically in combinatorial commutative algebra, a convex lattice polytope P is called _____ if it has the following property: given any positive integer n, every lattice point of the dilation nP, obtained from P by scaling its vertices by the factor n and taking the convex hull of the resulting points, can be written as the sum of exactly n lattice points in P. This property plays an important role in the theory of toric varieties, where it corresponds to projective normality of the toric variety determined by P.

The simplex in R^k with the vertices at the origin and along the unit coordinate vectors is _____.

a. Demihypercubes
b. Normal
c. Polytetrahedron
d. Hypercube

54. The _____ is an important family of continuous probability distributions, applicable in many fields. Each member of the family may be defined by two parameters, location and scale: the mean and variance respectively. The standard _____ is the _____ with a mean of zero and a variance of one.

a. Null hypothesis
b. Normal distribution
c. Coefficient of variation
d. Percentile rank

55. An _____ is a survey of public opinion from a particular sample. _____s are usually designed to represent the opinions of a population by conducting a series of questions and then extrapolating generalities in ratio or within confidence intervals.

The first known example of an _____ was a local straw poll conducted by The Harrisburg Pennsylvanian in 1824, showing Andrew Jackson leading John Quincy Adams by 335 votes to 169 in the contest for the United States Presidency.

a. A Mathematical Theory of Communication
b. A posteriori
c. Opinion poll
d. A chemical equation

Chapter 8. Data Description and Probability Distributions

56. In probability theory, a probability distribution is called _____ if its cumulative distribution function is _____. That is equivalent to saying that for random variables X with the distribution in question, Pr[X = a] = 0 for all real numbers a. If the distribution of X is _____ then X is called a _____ random variable.
    a. Concatenated codes
    b. Continuous phase modulation
    c. Continuous
    d. Conull set

57. _____ is a quantity expressing the two-dimensional size of a defined part of a surface, typically a region bounded by a closed curve. The term surface _____ refers to the total _____ of the exposed surface of a 3-dimensional solid, such as the sum of the _____s of the exposed sides of a polyhedron. _____ is an important invariant in the differential geometry of surfaces.
    a. A Mathematical Theory of Communication
    b. A chemical equation
    c. A posteriori
    d. Area

58. _____ consists of 'social relations involving authority or power' and refers to the regulation of a political unit, and to the methods and tactics used to formulate and apply policy.

    Political science (also political studies) is the study of political behavior, and examines the acquisition and application of power. Related areas of study include political philosophy, which seeks a rationale for _____ and an ethic of public behavior, and public administration, which examines the practices of governance.

    a. 2-3 heap
    b. Politics
    c. 120-cell
    d. 1-center problem

59. In mathematics, the _____ is an approach to finding a particular solution to certain inhomogeneous ordinary differential equations and recurrence relations. It is closely related to the annihilator method, but instead of using a particular kind of differential operator in order to find the best possible form of the particular solution, a 'guess' is made as to the appropriate form, which is then tested by differentiating the resulting equation. In this sense, the _____ is less formal but more intuitive than the annihilator method.
    a. Phase line
    b. Differential algebraic equations
    c. Linear differential equation
    d. Method of undetermined coefficients

Chapter 9. Games and Decisions

1. A _____ is a structured activity, usually undertaken for enjoyment and sometimes also used as an educational tool. _____s are distinct from work, which is usually carried out for remuneration, and from art, which is more concerned with the expression of ideas. However, the distinction is not clear-cut, and many _____s are also considered to be work (such as professional players of spectator sports/_____s) or art (such as jigsaw puzzles or _____s involving an artistic layout such as Mah-jongg solitaire.)
   a. Game
   b. 120-cell
   c. 1-center problem
   d. 2-3 heap

2. _____ is a branch of applied mathematics that is used in the social sciences, biology, engineering, political science, international relations, computer science, and philosophy. _____ attempts to mathematically capture behavior in strategic situations, in which an individual's success in making choices depends on the choices of others. While initially developed to analyze competitions in which one individual does better at another's expense, it has been expanded to treat a wide class of interactions, which are classified according to several criteria.
   a. Consumer theory
   b. Computational economic
   c. Mathematical economics
   d. Game theory

3. In mathematics, a _____ is a rectangular table of elements, which may be numbers or, more generally, any abstract quantities that can be added and multiplied. Matrices are used to describe linear equations, keep track of the coefficients of linear transformations and to record data that depend on multiple parameters. Matrices are described by the field of _____ theory.
   a. Coherent
   b. Matrix
   c. Compression
   d. Double counting

4. The word _____ has many distinct meanings in different fields of knowledge, depending on their methodologies and the context of discussion. Broadly speaking we can say that a _____ is some kind of belief or claim that (supposedly) explains, asserts, or consolidates some class of claims. Additionally, in contrast with a theorem the statement of the _____ is generally accepted only in some tentative fashion as opposed to regarding it as having been conclusively established.
   a. Defined
   b. Per mil
   c. Transport of structure
   d. Theory

5. In game theory, a player's _____ in a game is a complete plan of action for whatever situation might arise; this fully determines the player's behaviour. A player's _____ will determine the action the player will take at any stage of the game, for every possible history of play up to that stage.

A _____ profile is a set of strategies for each player which fully specifies all actions in a game.

   a. Matching pennies
   b. Correlated equilibrium
   c. Sir Philip Sidney game
   d. Strategy

6. In probability theory and statistics, the _____ of a random variable is the integral of the random variable with respect to its probability measure. For discrete random variables this is equivalent to the probability-weighted sum of the possible values, and for continuous random variables with a density function it is the probability density-weighted integral of the possible values.

The _____ may be intuitively understood by the law of large numbers: The _____, when it exists, is almost surely the limit of the sample mean as sample size grows to infinity.

   a. Illustration
   b. Infinitely divisible distribution
   c. Expected value
   d. Event

7. In mathematics, a _____ is a statement that can be proved on the basis of explicitly stated or previously agreed assumptions.
   a. Logical value
   b. Theorem
   c. Disjunction introduction
   d. Boolean function

8. In mathematics, _____ is a technique for optimization of a linear objective function, subject to linear equality and linear inequality constraints. Informally, _____ determines the way to achieve the best outcome in a given mathematical model given some list of requirements represented as linear equations.

More formally, given a polytope, and a real-valued affine function

$$f(x_1, x_2, \ldots, x_n) = c_1 x_1 + c_2 x_2 + \cdots + c_n x_n + d$$

defined on this polytope, a _____ method will find a point in the polytope where this function has the smallest value.

   a. Descent direction
   b. Linear programming relaxation
   c. Linear programming
   d. Lin-Kernighan

9. In geometry, a _____ or n-_____ is an n-dimensional analogue of a triangle. Specifically, a _____ is the convex hull of a set of affinely independent points in some Euclidean space of dimension n or higher.

For example, a 0-_____ is a point, a 1-_____ is a line segment, a 2-_____ is a triangle, a 3-_____ is a tetrahedron, and a 4-_____ is a pentachoron.

   a. Simplex
   b. Hypercell
   c. Polytetrahedron
   d. Demihypercubes

10. In mathematical optimization theory, the simplex algorithm, created by the American mathematician George Dantzig in 1947, is a popular algorithm for numerical solution of the linear programming problem. The journal Computing in Science and Engineering listed it as one of the top 10 algorithms of the century.

An unrelated, but similarly named method is the Nelder-Mead method or downhill _____ due to Nelder ' Mead and is a numerical method for optimising many-dimensional unconstrained problems, belonging to the more general class of search algorithms.

   a. Differential evolution
   b. Fibonacci search
   c. Hill climbing
   d. Simplex method

Chapter 10. Markov Chains

1. In mathematics, a _____, named after Andrey Markov, is a stochastic process with the Markov property. Having the Markov property means that, given the present state, future states are independent of the past states. In other words, the description of the present state fully captures all the information that could influence the future evolution of the process. Future states will be reached through a probabilistic process instead of a deterministic one.
   a. Law of Truly Large Numbers
   b. Variance-to-mean ratio
   c. Possibility theory
   d. Markov chain

2. A _____ is the counterpart to a deterministic process in probability theory. Instead of dealing with only one possible 'reality' of how the process might evolve under time, in a stochastic or random process there is some indeterminacy in its future evolution described by probability distributions. This means that even if the initial condition is known, there are many possibilities the process might go to, but some paths are more probable and others less.
   a. Mixing time
   b. Stochastic process
   c. Stochastic simulation
   d. Fractional Brownian motion

3. A _____ is a 2D geometric symbolic representation of information according to some visualization technique. Sometimes, the technique uses a 3D visualization which is then projected onto the 2D surface. The word graph is sometimes used as a synonym for _____.
   a. Diagram
   b. 1-center problem
   c. 120-cell
   d. 2-3 heap

4. In differential geometry, a discipline within mathematics, a _____ is a subset of the tangent bundle of a manifold satisfying certain properties. _____s are used to build up notions of integrability, and specifically of a foliation of a manifold
   a. Constraint
   b. Coherence
   c. Discontinuity
   d. Distribution

5. In mathematics, a _____ is a rectangular table of elements, which may be numbers or, more generally, any abstract quantities that can be added and multiplied. Matrices are used to describe linear equations, keep track of the coefficients of linear transformations and to record data that depend on multiple parameters. Matrices are described by the field of _____ theory.

a. Compression
b. Coherent
c. Double counting
d. Matrix

6. _____ is the likelihood or chance that something is the case or will happen. Theoretical _____ is used extensively in areas such as statistics, mathematics, science and philosophy to draw conclusions about the likelihood of potential events and the underlying mechanics of complex systems.

The word _____ does not have a consistent direct definition.

a. Standardized moment
b. Probability
c. Statistical significance
d. Discrete random variable

7. In mathematics, a stochastic matrix, probability matrix, or _____ is used to describe the transitions of a Markov chain. It has found use in probability theory, statistics and linear algebra, as well as computer science. There are several different definitions and types of stochastic matrices;

A right stochastic matrix is a square matrix each of whose rows consists of nonnegative real numbers, with each row summing to 1.

a. Pick matrix
b. Hessenberg matrix
c. Transition matrix
d. Sylvester matrix

8. _____, in mathematics and computer science, is a method of defining functions in which the function being defined is applied within its own definition. The term is also used more generally to describe a process of repeating objects in a self-similar way. For instance, when the surfaces of two mirrors are almost parallel with each other the nested images that occur are a form of _____.
a. 1-center problem
b. Recursion
c. 2-3 heap
d. 120-cell

9. In mathematics, _____ is the operation of adding two matrices by adding the corresponding entries together. However, there is another operation which could also be considered as a kind of addition for matrices.

The usual _____ is defined for two matrices of the same dimensions.

 a. Spectral theory
 b. Standard basis
 c. Jordan normal form
 d. Matrix addition

10. _____ is an important tool for manufacturing and engineering, where it can have a major impact on the productivity of a process. In manufacturing, the purpose of _____ is to minimize the production time and costs, by telling a production facility what to make, when, with which staff, and on which equipment. Production _____ aims to maximize the efficiency of the operation and reduce costs.
 a. Boolean algebra
 b. Crib
 c. Critical point
 d. Scheduling

11. The term '_____' refers to the concept of collecting information and attempting to spot a pattern in the information. In some fields of study, the term '_____' has more formally-defined meanings.

Although _____ is often used to predict future events, it could be used to estimate uncertain events in the past, such as how many ancient kings probably ruled between two dates, based on data such as the average years which other known kings reigned.

 a. Probit model
 b. Partial least squares
 c. Partial leverage
 d. Trend analysis

12. _____ Any process by which a specified characteristic usually amplitude of the output of a device is prevented from exceeding a predetermined value.
 a. Logical equivalence
 b. Parametric continuity
 c. Notation
 d. Limiting

13. _____ , a discipline of biology, is the science of heredity and variation in living organisms. The fact that living things inherit traits from their parents has been used since prehistoric times to improve crop plants and animals through selective breeding. However, the modern science of _____, which seeks to understand the process of inheritance, only began with the work of Gregor Mendel in the mid-nineteenth century.

   a. Hardy-Weinberg principle
   b. Polytomy
   c. Genetics
   d. Fitness landscapes

14. _____ consists of 'social relations involving authority or power' and refers to the regulation of a political unit, and to the methods and tactics used to formulate and apply policy.

Political science (also political studies) is the study of political behavior, and examines the acquisition and application of power. Related areas of study include political philosophy, which seeks a rationale for _____ and an ethic of public behavior, and public administration, which examines the practices of governance.

   a. 120-cell
   b. 1-center problem
   c. 2-3 heap
   d. Politics

15. _____ is a legal term (in some jurisdictions, notably in the USA, United Kingdom, Canada, and Australia) that encompasses land along with anything permanently affixed to the land, such as buildings, specifically property that is stationary, or fixed in location. _____ law is the body of regulations and legal codes which pertain to such matters under a particular jurisdiction. _____ is often considered synonymous with real property (also sometimes called realty), in contrast with personal property (also sometimes called chattel or personalty under chattel law or personal property law.)

   a. Real estate
   b. Home equity
   c. 120-cell
   d. 1-center problem

16. In classical differential geometry, _____ refers to the simple idea of rolling one smooth surface over another in Euclidean space. For example, the tangent plane to a surface at a point can be rolled around the surface to obtain the tangent-plane at other points.

The tangential contact between the surfaces being rolled over one another provides a relation between points on the two surfaces.

a. Development
b. Blinding
c. Double counting
d. FISH

17. _____, also sometimes known as standard form or as exponential notation, is a way of writing numbers that accommodates values too large or small to be conveniently written in standard decimal notation. _____ has a number of useful properties and is often favored by scientists, mathematicians and engineers, who work with such numbers.

In _____, numbers are written in the form:

$$a \times 10^b$$

a. Radix point
b. 1-center problem
c. Leading zero
d. Scientific notation

1. _____s is the social science that studies the production, distribution, and consumption of goods and services.

The term _____s comes from the Ancient Greek oá¼°κονομῖα (oikonomia, 'management of a household, administration') from oá¼¶κος (oikos, 'house') + νΌξμος (nomos, 'custom' or 'law'), hence 'rules of the house(hold)'.

Current _____ models developed out of the broader field of political economy in the late 19th century, owing to a desire to use an empirical approach more akin to the physical sciences.

   a. A Mathematical Theory of Communication
   b. A chemical equation
   c. Experimental economics
   d. Economic

2. The _____ are the set of numbers consisting of the natural numbers including 0 and their negatives. They are numbers that can be written without a fractional or decimal component, and fall within the set {... −2, −1, 0, 1, 2, ...}.
   a. A Mathematical Theory of Communication
   b. Integers
   c. A posteriori
   d. A chemical equation

3. In mathematics, a _____ can mean either an element of the set {1, 2, 3, ...} or an element of the set {0, 1, 2, 3, ...}. The latter is especially preferred in mathematical logic, set theory, and computer science.

_____s have two main purposes: they can be used for counting, and they can be used for ordering.

   a. Cardinal numbers
   b. Natural number
   c. Suslin cardinal
   d. Strong partition cardinal

4. In mathematics, a _____ is any function which can be written as the ratio of two polynomial functions. _____ of degree 2 :

$$y = \frac{x^2 - 3x - 2}{x^2 - 4}$$

Chapter 11. Basic Algebra Review

In the case of one variable, x, a _____ is a function of the form

$$f(x) = \frac{P(x)}{Q(x)}$$

where P and Q are polynomial function in x and Q is not the zero polynomial. The domain of f is the set of all points x for which the denominator Q

- a. 120-cell
- b. 1-center problem
- c. Legendre rational functions
- d. Rational function

5. In mathematics, a _____ is a number which can be expressed as a ratio of two integers. Non-integer _____s are usually written as the vulgar fraction $\frac{a}{b}$, where b is not zero. a is called the numerator, and b the denominator.
- a. Tally marks
- b. Rational number
- c. Minkowski distance
- d. Pre-algebra

6. In mathematics, the _____s may be described informally in several different ways. The _____s include both rational numbers, such as 42 and −23/129, and irrational numbers, such as pi and the square root of two; or, a _____ can be given by an infinite decimal representation, such as 2.4871773339...., where the digits continue in some way; or, the _____s may be thought of as points on an infinitely long number line.

These descriptions of the _____s, while intuitively accessible, are not sufficiently rigorous for the purposes of pure mathematics.

- a. Pre-algebra
- b. Tally marks
- c. Minkowski distance
- d. Real number

7. The mathematical concept of a _____ expresses the intuitive idea of deterministic dependence between two quantities, one of which is viewed as primary and the other as secondary. A _____ then is a way to associate a unique output for each input of a specified type, for example, a real number or an element of a given set.

a. Coherent
b. Grill
c. Function
d. Going up

8. In mathematics the _____ of a set which is equipped with the operation of addition is an element which, when added to any element x in the set, yields x. One of the most familiar additive identities is the number 0 from elementary mathematics, but additive identities occur in other mathematical structures where addition is defined, such as in groups and rings.

- The _____ familiar from elementary mathematics is zero, denoted 0. For example,

    5 + 0 = 5 = 0 + 5.

- In the natural numbers N and all of its supersets, the _____ is 0. Thus for any one of these numbers n,

    n + 0 = n = 0 + n.

Let N be a set which is closed under the operation of addition, denoted +. An _____ for N is any element e such that for any element n in N,

e + n = n = n + e.

a. Unit ring
b. Algebraically independent
c. Unique factorization domain
d. Additive identity

9. In mathematics, the _____ of a number n is the number that, when added to n, yields zero. The _____ of n is denoted −n. For example, 7 is −7, because 7 + (−7) = 0, and the _____ of −0.3 is 0.3, because −0.3 + 0.3 = 0.
a. Additive inverse
b. Algebraic structure
c. Arity
d. Associativity

10. _____ is the mathematical operation of scaling one number by another. It is one of the four basic operations in elementary arithmetic.

Chapter 11. Basic Algebra Review

_____ is defined for whole numbers in terms of repeated addition; for example, 4 multiplied by 3 can be calculated by adding 3 copies of 4 together:

$$4 + 4 + 4 = 12.$$

_____ of rational numbers and real numbers is defined by systematic generalization of this basic idea.

a. The number 0 is even.
b. Least common multiple
c. Highest common factor
d. Multiplication

11. In mathematics, the term _____ has several different important meanings:

- An _____ is an equality that remains true regardless of the values of any variables that appear within it, to distinguish it from an equality which is true under more particular conditions. For this, the 'triple bar' symbol ≡ is sometimes used.
- In algebra, an _____ or _____ element of a set S with a binary operation Â· is an element e that, when combined with any element x of S, produces that same x. That is, eÂ·x = xÂ·e = x for all x in S.
    - The _____ function from a set S to itself, often denoted id or id$_S$, s the function such that i = x for all x in S. This function serves as the _____ element in the set of all functions from S to itself with respect to function composition.
    - In linear algebra, the _____ matrix of size n is the n-by-n square matrix with ones on the main diagonal and zeros elsewhere. This matrix serves as the _____ with respect to matrix multiplication.

A common example of the first meaning is the trigonometric _____

$$\sin^2 \theta + \cos^2 \theta = 1$$

which is true for all real values of θ, as opposed to

$$\cos \theta = 1,$$

which is true only for some values of θ, not all. For example, the latter equation is true when $\theta = 0$, false when $\theta = 2$

The concepts of 'additive _____' and 'multiplicative _____' are central to the Peano axioms. The number 0 is the 'additive _____' for integers, real numbers, and complex numbers. For the real numbers, for all $a \in \mathbb{R}$,

$$0 + a = a,$$

$$a + 0 = a, \text{ and}$$

$$0 + 0 = 0.$$

Similarly, The number 1 is the 'multiplicative _____' for integers, real numbers, and complex numbers.

   a. Intersection
   b. Action
   c. Identity
   d. ARIA

12. In mathematics, a _____ is a picture of a straight line in which the integers are shown as specially-marked points evenly spaced on the line. Although this image only shows the integers from -9 to 9, the line includes all real numbers, continuing 'forever' in each direction. It is often used as an aid in teaching simple addition and subtraction, especially involving negative numbers.
   a. Number system
   b. Point plotting
   c. Real number
   d. Number line

13. In mathematics, the _____ of a Euclidean space is a special point, usually denoted by the letter O, used as a fixed point of reference for the geometry of the surrounding space. In a Cartesian coordinate system, the _____ is the point where the axes of the system intersect. In Euclidean geometry, the _____ may be chosen freely as any convenient point of reference.
   a. Interval
   b. Autonomous system
   c. OMAC
   d. Origin

Chapter 11. Basic Algebra Review

14. In mathematics, _____ is a property that a binary operation can have. It means that, within an expression containing two or more of the same associative operators in a row, the order that the operations are performed does not matter as long as the sequence of the operands is not changed. That is, rearranging the parentheses in such an expression will not change its value.
    a. Algebraically closed
    b. Unital
    c. Associativity
    d. Idempotence

15. The _____ is a rule which states that when you add or multiply numbers, changing the order doesn't change the result.
    a. Coimage
    b. Semigroupoid
    c. Conditional event algebra
    d. Commutative law

16. In mathematics, an _____ is a special type of element of a set with respect to a binary operation on that set. It leaves other elements unchanged when combined with them. This is used for groups and related concepts.
    a. Algebraically closed
    b. Universal algebra
    c. Arity
    d. Identity element

17. In mathematics, a _____ for a number x, denoted by $1/x$ or x^{-1}, is a number which when multiplied by x yields the multiplicative identity, 1. The _____ of x is also called the reciprocal of x. The _____ of a fraction p/q is q/p.
    a. Hyperbolic function
    b. Golden function
    c. Double exponential
    d. Multiplicative inverse

18. In mathematics, an _____ or member of a set is any one of the distinct objects that make up that set.

Writing A = {1,2,3,4}, means that the _____s of the set A are the numbers 1, 2, 3 and 4. Groups of _____s of A, for example {1,2}, are subsets of A.

a. Ideal
b. Universal code
c. Order
d. Element

19. In mathematics, and in particular in abstract algebra, distributivity is a property of binary operations that generalises the _____ law from elementary algebra.

a. Closure with a twist
b. Distributive
c. General linear group
d. Permutation

20. In mathematics, the multiplicative inverse of a number x, denoted 1/x or x^{-1}, is the number which, when multiplied by x, yields 1. The multiplicative inverse of x is also called the _____ of x.

a. 120-cell
b. 2-3 heap
c. 1-center problem
d. Reciprocal

21. In abstract algebra, a field extension L /K is called _____ if every element of L is _____ over K. Field extensions which are not _____.

For example, the field extension R/Q, that is the field of real numbers as an extension of the field of rational numbers, is transcendental, while the field extensions C/R and Q

a. Echo
b. Ideal
c. Identity
d. Algebraic

22. In mathematics and computer science, _____ (also base-16, hexa or base, of 16. It uses sixteen distinct symbols, most often the symbols 0-9 to represent values zero to nine, and A, B, C, D, E, F (or a through f) to represent values ten to fifteen.

Its primary use is as a human friendly representation of binary coded values, so it is often used in digital electronics and computer engineering.

Chapter 11. Basic Algebra Review

a. Radix
b. Hexadecimal
c. Factoradic
d. Tetradecimal

23. The _____ is the sum of the exponents of the variables in the term.
   a. Contract curve
   b. Biscuspid
   c. Bar product
   d. Degree of a term

24. In mathematics, a _____ is an expression constructed from variables and constants, using the operations of addition, subtraction, multiplication, and constant non-negative whole number exponents. For example, $x^2 - 4x + 7$ is a _____, but $x^2 - 4/x + 7x^{3/2}$ is not, because its second term involves division by the variable x and also because its third term contains an exponent that is not a whole number.

_____s are one of the most important concepts in algebra and throughout mathematics and science.

   a. Coimage
   b. Group extension
   c. Semifield
   d. Polynomial

25. Exponentiation is a mathematical operation, written a^n, involving two numbers, the base a and the _____ n. When n is a positive integer, exponentiation corresponds to repeated multiplication:

$$a^n = \underbrace{a \times \cdots \times a}_{n},$$

just as multiplication by a positive integer corresponds to repeated addition:

$$a \times n = \underbrace{a + \cdots + a}_{n}.$$

The _____ is usually shown as a superscript to the right of the base. The exponentiation a^n can be read as: a raised to the n-th power, a raised to the power [of] n or possibly a raised to the _____ [of] n, or more briefly: a to the n-th power or a to the power [of] n, or even more briefly: a to the n.

a. Exponential sum
b. Exponential tree
c. Exponentiating by squaring
d. Exponent

26. In elementary algebra, a _____ is a polynomial with two terms: the sum of two monomials. It is the simplest kind of polynomial except for a monomial.

The _____ $a^2 - b^2$ can be factored as the product of two other _____s:

   $a^2 - b^2$.

The product of a pair of linear _____s a x + b and c x + d is:

   2 +x + bd.

A _____ raised to the nth power, represented as

   n

can be expanded by means of the _____ theorem or, equivalently, using Pascal's triangle.

a. Real structure
b. Cylindrical algebraic decomposition
c. Binomial
d. Rational root theorem

27. In mathematics, a _____ is a constant multiplicative factor of a certain object. For example, in the expression $9x^2$, the _____ of x^2 is 9.

The object can be such things as a variable, a vector, a function, etc.

a. Fibonacci polynomials
b. Multivariate division algorithm
c. Coefficient
d. Stability radius

28. In mathematics, the word _____ means two different things in the context of polynomials:

- The first meaning is a product of powers of variables, or formally any value obtained from 1 by finitely many multiplications by a variable. If only a single variable x is considered this means that any _____ is either 1 or a power x^n of x, with n a positive integer. If several variables are considered, say, x, y, z, then each can be given an exponent, so that any _____ is of the form $x^a y^b z^c$ with a,b,c nonnegative integers.
- The second meaning of _____ includes _____s in the first sense, but also allows multiplication by any constant, so that $-7x^5$ and $4yz^{13}$ are also considered to be _____s.

With either definition, the set of _____s is a subset of all polynomials that is closed under multiplication.

  a. Power sum symmetric polynomial
  b. Monomial
  c. Homogeneous polynomial
  d. Diagonal form

29. In vascular plants, the _____ is the organ of a plant body that typically lies below the surface of the soil. This is not always the case, however, since a _____ can also be aerial (that is, growing above the ground) or aerating (that is, growing up above the ground or especially above water.) Furthermore, a stem normally occurring below ground is not exceptional either
  a. Root
  b. 2-3 heap
  c. 1-center problem
  d. 120-cell

30. In elementary algebra, a _____ is a polynomial consisting of three terms; in other words, a _____ is the sum of three monomials. It can be factored using simple steps

In linguistics, a _____ is a fixed expression which is made from three words; e.g. 'lights, camera, action', 'signed, sealed, delivered'.

  a. Relation algebra
  b. Recurrence relation
  c. Trinomial
  d. Symmetric difference

31. A _____ of a number is a number a such that $a^3 = x$.

a. Golden function
b. Square root
c. Hyperbolic functions
d. Cube root

32. In mathematics and in the sciences, a _____ (plural: _____e, formulæ or _____s) is a concise way of expressing information symbolically (as in a mathematical or chemical _____), or a general relationship between quantities. One of many famous _____e is Albert Einstein's E = mc² (see special relativity

In mathematics, a _____ is a key to solve an equation with variables. For example, the problem of determining the volume of a sphere is one that requires a significant amount of integral calculus to solve.

a. 2-3 heap
b. 120-cell
c. 1-center problem
d. Formula

33. In abstract algebra, a module S over a ring R is called _____ or irreducible if it is not the zero module 0 and if its only submodules are 0 and S. Understanding the _____ modules over a ring is usually helpful because these modules form the 'building blocks' of all other modules in a certain sense.

Abelian groups are the same as Z-modules.

a. Basis
b. Simple
c. Harmonic series
d. Derivation

34. _____, also sometimes known as standard form or as exponential notation, is a way of writing numbers that accommodates values too large or small to be conveniently written in standard decimal notation. _____ has a number of useful properties and is often favored by scientists, mathematicians and engineers, who work with such numbers.

In _____, numbers are written in the form:

$$a \times 10^b$$

Chapter 11. Basic Algebra Review

   a. Scientific notation
   b. Radix point
   c. 1-center problem
   d. Leading zero

35. In mathematics, specifically in combinatorial commutative algebra, a convex lattice polytope P is called _____ if it has the following property: given any positive integer n, every lattice point of the dilation nP, obtained from P by scaling its vertices by the factor n and taking the convex hull of the resulting points, can be written as the sum of exactly n lattice points in P. This property plays an important role in the theory of toric varieties, where it corresponds to projective normality of the toric variety determined by P.

The simplex in R^k with the vertices at the origin and along the unit coordinate vectors is _____.

   a. Hypercube
   b. Normal
   c. Polytetrahedron
   d. Demihypercubes

36. The _____ is an important family of continuous probability distributions, applicable in many fields. Each member of the family may be defined by two parameters, location and scale: the mean and variance respectively. The standard _____ is the _____ with a mean of zero and a variance of one.
   a. Coefficient of variation
   b. Normal distribution
   c. Null hypothesis
   d. Percentile rank

37. In mathematics, an algebraic group G contains a unique maximal normal solvable subgroup; and this subgroup is closed. Its identity component is called the _____ of G.
   a. Block size
   b. Composite
   c. Barycentric coordinates
   d. Radical

38. In mathematics, a _____ of a number x is a number r such that $r^2 = x$, or, in other words, a number r whose square is x. Every non-negative real number x has a unique non-negative _____, called the principal _____, which is denoted with a radical symbol as $\sqrt{x}$, or, using exponent notation, as $x^{1/2}$. For example, the principal _____ of 9 is 3, denoted $\sqrt{9}$ = 3, because $3^2 = 3 \times 3 = 9$.

a. Square root
b. Hyperbolic functions
c. Double exponential
d. Multiplicative inverse

39. _____ is that which is owed; usually referencing assets owed, but the term can cover other obligations. In the case of assets, _____ is a means of using future purchasing power in the present before a summation has been earned.
  a. Point-slope form
  b. Metaheuristic
  c. Cobb-Douglas
  d. Debt

40. The _____ of a material is defined as its mass per unit volume:

$$\rho = \frac{m}{V}$$

Different materials usually have different densities, so _____ is an important concept regarding buoyancy, metal purity and packaging.

In some cases _____ is expressed as the dimensionless quantities specific gravity or relative _____, in which case it is expressed in multiples of the _____ of some other standard material, usually water or air.

In a well-known story, Archimedes was given the task of determining whether King Hiero's goldsmith was embezzling gold during the manufacture of a wreath dedicated to the gods and replacing it with another, cheaper alloy.

  a. 2-3 heap
  b. Density
  c. 120-cell
  d. 1-center problem

41. In differential geometry, a discipline within mathematics, a _____ is a subset of the tangent bundle of a manifold satisfying certain properties. _____s are used to build up notions of integrability, and specifically of a foliation of a manifold

a. Discontinuity
b. Constraint
c. Coherence
d. Distribution

42. A _____ is an algebraic equation in which each term is either a constant or the product of a constant and a single variable. _____s can have one, two, three or more variables.

_____s occur with great regularity in applied mathematics.

a. Quartic equation
b. Linear equation
c. Difference of two squares
d. Quadratic equation

43. In the study of metric spaces in mathematics, there are various notions of two metrics on the same underlying space being 'the same', or _____.

In the following, M will denote a non-empty set and d_1 and d_2 will denote two metrics on M.

The two metrics d_1 and d_2 are said to be topologically _____ if they generate the same topology on M.

a. Equivalent
b. A Mathematical Theory of Communication
c. A posteriori
d. A chemical equation

44. In mathematics, a _____ is a set of real numbers with the property that any number that lies between two numbers in the set is also included in the set. For example, the set of all numbers x satisfying $0 \leq x \leq 1$ is an _____ which contains 0 and 1, as well as all numbers between them. Other examples of _____s are the set of all real numbers $\mathbb{R}$, the set of all positive real numbers, and the empty set.

a. Order
b. Interval
c. Annihilator
d. Ideal

45. _____ is the notation in which permitted values for a variable are expressed as ranging over a certain interval; "5 < x < 9" is an example of the application of _____.
   a. A Mathematical Theory of Communication
   b. Infinity
   c. Implicit differentiation
   d. Interval notation

46. In mathematics, an _____ is a statement about the relative size or order of two objects, or about whether they are the same or not

- The notation a < b means that a is less than b.
- The notation a > b means that a is greater than b.
- The notation a ≠ b means that a is not equal to b, but does not say that one is bigger than the other or even that they can be compared in size.

In all these cases, a is not equal to b, hence, '_____'.

These relations are known as strict _____

- The notation a ≤ b means that a is less than or equal to b;
- The notation a ≥ b means that a is greater than or equal to b;

An additional use of the notation is to show that one quantity is much greater than another, normally by several orders of magnitude.

- The notation a << b means that a is much less than b.
- The notation a >> b means that a is much greater than b.

If the sense of the _____ is the same for all values of the variables for which its members are defined, then the _____ is called an 'absolute' or 'unconditional' _____. If the sense of an _____ holds only for certain values of the variables involved, but is reversed or destroyed for other values of the variables, it is called a conditional _____.

An _____ may appear unsolvable because it only states whether a number is larger or smaller than another number; but it is possible to apply the same operations for equalities to inequalities. For example, to find x for the _____ 10x > 23 one would divide 23 by 10.

   a. Inequality
   b. A posteriori
   c. A chemical equation
   d. A Mathematical Theory of Communication

Chapter 11. Basic Algebra Review

47. In a graph theory, the _____ L

One of the earliest and most important theorems about _____s is due to Hassler Whitney, who proved that with one exceptional case the structure of G can be recovered completely from its _____.

   a. Sparse graph
   b. Line graph
   c. Vertex-transitive graph
   d. Bivariegated graph

48. In economics, business, retail, and accounting, a _____ is the value of money that has been used up to produce something, and hence is not available for use anymore. In business, the _____ may be one of acquisition, in which case the amount of money expended to acquire it is counted as _____. In this case, money is the input that is gone in order to acquire the thing.
   a. 120-cell
   b. 2-3 heap
   c. 1-center problem
   d. Cost

49. In mathematics, a _____ is the end result of a division problem. It can also be expressed as the number of times the divisor divides into the dividend.
   a. Notation
   b. Marginal cost
   c. Limiting
   d. Quotient

50. In mathematics, a _____ is a polynomial equation of the second degree. The general form is

$$ax^2 + bx + c = 0,$$

where a ≠ 0.

The letters a, b, and c are called coefficients: the quadratic coefficient a is the coefficient of x^2, the linear coefficient b is the coefficient of x, and c is the constant coefficient, also called the free term or constant term.

a. Difference of two squares
b. Quartic equation
c. Quadratic equation
d. Linear equation

51. In algebra, the _____ of a polynomial with real or complex coefficients is a certain expression in the coefficients of the polynomial which is equal to zero if and only if the polynomial has a multiple root in the complex numbers. For example, the _____ of the quadratic polynomial

$$ax^2 + bx + c \text{ is } b^2 - 4ac.$$

The _____ of the cubic polynomial

$$ax^3 + bx^2 + cx + d \text{ is } b^2c^2 - 4ac^3 - 4b^3d - 27a^2d^2 + 18abcd.$$

a. Square-free polynomial
b. Jacobian conjecture
c. Boubaker polynomial
d. Discriminant

52. _____ is an algebraic technique used to solve quadratic equations, in analytic geometry for determining the shapes of graphs, and in calculus for computing integrals. The essential objective is to reduce a quadratic polynomial in a variable in an equation or expression to a squared polynomial of linear order. This can reduce an equation or integral to one that is more easily solved or evaluated.
a. Relation algebra
b. Permanent of a matrix
c. Monomial basis
d. Completing the square

53. A quadratic equation with real solutions, called roots, which may be real or complex, is given by the _____: $x = \frac{-b \pm \sqrt{b^2 - 4ac}}{2a}$.
a. Differential Algebra
b. Quotient
c. Parametric continuity
d. Quadratic formula

Chapter 11. Basic Algebra Review

54. In mathematics, a _____ is a statement that can be proved on the basis of explicitly stated or previously agreed assumptions.
    a. Logical value
    b. Boolean function
    c. Theorem
    d. Disjunction introduction

55. In mathematics, the point $\tilde{\mathbf{x}} \in \mathbb{R}^n$ is an _____ for the differential equation

$$\frac{d\mathbf{x}}{dt} = \mathbf{f}(t, \mathbf{x})$$

if $\mathbf{f}(t, \tilde{\mathbf{x}}) = 0$ for all t.

Similarly, the point $\tilde{\mathbf{x}} \in \mathbb{R}^n$ is an _____ for the difference equation

$$\mathbf{x}_{k+1} = \mathbf{f}(k, \mathbf{x}_k)$$

if $\mathbf{f}(k, \tilde{\mathbf{x}}) = \tilde{\mathbf{x}}$ for $k = 0, 1, 2, \ldots$.

Equilibria can be classified by looking at the signs of the eigenvalues of the linearization of the equations about the equilibria.

   a. Uniform algebra
   b. Unitary transformation
   c. Algorithm design
   d. Equilibrium point

56. _____ is an economic model describing effects on price and quantity in a market. It predicts that in a competitive market, price will function to equalize the quantity demanded by consumers, and the quantity supplied by producers, resulting in an economic equilibrium of price and quantity. The model incorporates other factors changing equilibrium as a shift of demand and/or supply.
   a. Cross price elasticity of demand
   b. 1-center problem
   c. Marginal rate of substitution
   d. Supply and demand

57. _____ is the concept of adding accumulated interest back to the principal, so that interest is earned on interest from that moment on. The act of declaring interest to be principal is called compounding. A loan, for example, may have its interest compounded every month: in this case, a loan with $100 principal and 1% interest per month would have a balance of $101 at the end of the first month.
   a. Net interest margin
   b. Net interest margin securities
   c. Retained interest
   d. Compound interest

58. _____ is a fee, paid on borrowed capital. Assets lent include money, shares, consumer goods through hire purchase, major assets such as aircraft, and even entire factories in finance lease arrangements. The _____ is calculated upon the value of the assets in the same manner as upon money.
   a. Interest sensitivity gap
   b. A Mathematical Theory of Communication
   c. Interest
   d. Interest expense

59. Leonardo of Pisa (c. 1170 - c. 1250), also known as Leonardo Pisano, Leonardo Bonacci, Leonardo _____, or, most commonly, simply _____, was an Italian mathematician, considered by some 'the most talented mathematician of the Middle Ages'.
   a. Harry Hinsley
   b. Ralph C. Merkle
   c. Guido Castelnuovo
   d. Fibonacci

60. In mathematics, a _____ is often represented as the sum of a sequence of terms. That is, a _____ is represented as a list of numbers with addition operations between them, for example this arithmetic sequence:

   $1 + 2 + 3 + 4 + 5 + ... + 99 + 100$

In most cases of interest the terms of the sequence are produced according to a certain rule, such as by a formula, by an algorithm, by a sequence of measurements, or even by a random number generator.

   a. Contact
   b. Concavity
   c. Blind
   d. Series

61. The sum of an _____ $a_0 + a_1 + a_2 + \dots$ is the limit of the sequence of partial sums

$$S_n = a_0 + a_1 + a_2 + \dots + a_n,$$

as $n \to \infty$, if that limit exists. If the limit exists and is finite, the series is said to converge; if it is infinite or does not exist, the series is said to diverge.

The easiest way that an _____ can converge is if all the a_n are zero for n sufficiently large. Such a series can be identified with a finite sum, so it is only infinite in a trivial sense.

However, _____ of nonzero terms can also converge, which resolves the mathematical side of several of Zeno's paradoxes.

   a. Archimedes' use of infinitesimals
   b. Uniform convergence
   c. Interpolation
   d. Infinite Series

62. _____ is the addition of a set of numbers; the result is their sum or total. An interim or present total of a _____ process is termed the running total. The 'numbers' to be summed may be natural numbers, complex numbers, matrices, or still more complicated objects.

   a. 2-3 heap
   b. 1-center problem
   c. 120-cell
   d. Summation

63. In statistics, _____ has two related meanings:

- the arithmetic _____.
- the expected value of a random variable, which is also called the population _____.

It is sometimes stated that the '_____' _____s average. This is incorrect if '_____' is taken in the specific sense of 'arithmetic _____' as there are different types of averages: the _____, median, and mode. For instance, average house prices almost always use the median value for the average.

For a real-valued random variable X, the _____ is the expectation of X.

a. Probability
b. Proportional hazards model
c. Statistical population
d. Mean

64. In mathematics and statistics, the _____ of a list of numbers is the sum of all of the list divided by the number of items in the list. If the list is a statistical population, then the mean of that population is called a population mean. If the list is a statistical sample, we call the resulting statistic a sample mean.
   a. Unsolved problems in statistics
   b. Analysis of variance
   c. Interval estimation
   d. Arithmetic mean

65. In mathematics, an _____, or central tendency of a data set refers to a measure of the 'middle' or 'expected' value of the data set. There are many different descriptive statistics that can be chosen as a measurement of the central tendency of the data items.

An _____ is a single value that is meant to typify a list of values.

   a. A chemical equation
   b. Average
   c. A posteriori
   d. A Mathematical Theory of Communication

66. _____, in mathematics and computer science, is a method of defining functions in which the function being defined is applied within its own definition. The term is also used more generally to describe a process of repeating objects in a self-similar way. For instance, when the surfaces of two mirrors are almost parallel with each other the nested images that occur are a form of _____.
   a. 2-3 heap
   b. 1-center problem
   c. 120-cell
   d. Recursion

67. In mathematics, an arithmetic progression or _____ is a sequence of numbers such that the difference of any two successive members of the sequence is a constant. For instance, the sequence 3, 5, 7, 9, 11, 13... is an arithmetic progression with common difference 2.

a. Arithmetic sequence
b. Edgeworth series
c. Alternating series test
d. Eisenstein series

68. In mathematics, a _____ is a series with a constant ratio between successive terms. For example, the series

$$\frac{1}{2} + \frac{1}{4} + \frac{1}{8} + \frac{1}{16} + \cdots$$

is geometric, because each term is equal to half of the previous term. The sum of this series is 1, as illustrated in the following picture:

_____ are one of the simplest examples of infinite series with finite sums.

a. Summation by parts
b. Telescoping series
c. Riemann series theorem
d. Geometric series

69. In Fourier analysis, a _____ is a kind of linear operator, or transformation of functions. These operators multiply the Fourier coefficients of a function by a specified function, hence the name. Among the multipliers one can count some simple operators, such as translations and differentiation, but also some more complicated ones such as the convolutions, Hilbert transform, and others.

a. Reality condition
b. Modulated complex lapped transform
c. Fourier multiplier
d. Poisson summation formula

70. In mathematics, the _____ of a non-negative integer n, denoted by n!, is the product of all positive integers less than or equal to n. For example,

$$5! = 1 \times 2 \times 3 \times 4 \times 5 = 120$$

and

$$6! = 1 \times 2 \times 3 \times 4 \times 5 \times 6 = 720$$

The notation n! was introduced by Christian Kramp in 1808.

The _____ function is formally defined by

$$n! = \prod_{k=1}^{n} k \qquad \forall n \in \mathbb{N}.$$

The above definition incorporates the instance

$$0! = 1$$

as an instance of the fact that the product of no numbers at all is 1.

a. Symbolic combinatorics
b. Factorial
c. Plane partition
d. Partition of a set

71. In mathematics, the _____ is an important formula giving the expansion of powers of sums. Its simplest version states that

$$(x+y)^n = \sum_{k=0}^{n} \binom{n}{k} x^{n-k} y^k \qquad (1)$$

for any real or complex numbers x and y, and any nonnegative integer n. The binomial coefficient appearing in may be defined in terms of the factorial function n!:

$$\binom{n}{k} = \frac{n!}{k!(n-k)!}.$$

For example, here are the cases where $2 \le n \le 5$:

$$(x+y)^2 = x^2 + 2xy + y^2$$
$$(x+y)^3 = x^3 + 3x^2y + 3xy^2 + y^3$$
$$(x+y)^4 = x^4 + 4x^3y + 6x^2y^2 + 4xy^3 + y^4$$
$$(x+y)^5 = x^5 + 5x^4y + 10x^3y^2 + 10x^2y^3 + 5xy^4 + y^5.$$

Formula is valid more generally for any elements x and y of a semiring as long as xy = yx..

a. Hypergeometric identities
b. Stirling transform
c. Binomial theorem
d. Lah numbers

72. A _____ is one of the basic shapes of geometry: a polygon with three corners or vertices and three sides or edges which are line segments. A _____ with vertices A, B, and C is denoted ABC.

In Euclidean geometry any three non-collinear points determine a unique _____ and a unique plane.

a. Kepler triangle
b. 1-center problem
c. Fuhrmann circle
d. Triangle

73. _____ is a quantity expressing the two-dimensional size of a defined part of a surface, typically a region bounded by a closed curve. The term surface _____ refers to the total _____ of the exposed surface of a 3-dimensional solid, such as the sum of the _____s of the exposed sides of a polyhedron. _____ is an important invariant in the differential geometry of surfaces.
a. A Mathematical Theory of Communication
b. A posteriori
c. A chemical equation
d. Area

74. In mathematics, the concept of a _____ tries to capture the intuitive idea of a geometrical one-dimensional and continuous object. A simple example is the circle. In everyday use of the term '_____', a straight line is not curved, but in mathematical parlance _____s include straight lines and line segments.
a. Kappa curve
b. Negative pedal curve
c. Quadrifolium
d. Curve

Chapter 1

1. d	2. a	3. b	4. b	5. a	6. d	7. d	8. c	9. d	10. c
11. d	12. a	13. a	14. a	15. b	16. a	17. d	18. c	19. d	20. a
21. a	22. c	23. b	24. d	25. a	26. d	27. b	28. b	29. b	30. d
31. b	32. d	33. d	34. a	35. d	36. a	37. d	38. a	39. a	40. b
41. d	42. b	43. d	44. d	45. d	46. b	47. b	48. b	49. c	50. d
51. d	52. d	53. d							

Chapter 2

1. d	2. a	3. a	4. b	5. a	6. b	7. d	8. b	9. d	10. d
11. d	12. a	13. b	14. b	15. b	16. d	17. b	18. d	19. d	20. d
21. d	22. d	23. c	24. b	25. d	26. d	27. d	28. b	29. d	30. a
31. b	32. d	33. b	34. a	35. d	36. c	37. d	38. c	39. c	40. a
41. b	42. c	43. b	44. d	45. c					

Chapter 3

1. a	2. d	3. b	4. d	5. a	6. a	7. a	8. b	9. b	10. d
11. b	12. a	13. c	14. c	15. d	16. b	17. c			

Chapter 4

1. c	2. d	3. a	4. b	5. d	6. d	7. d	8. d	9. d	10. d
11. a	12. c	13. a	14. d	15. d	16. a	17. d	18. d	19. d	20. c
21. a	22. d	23. d	24. d	25. d	26. d	27. d	28. c	29. c	30. d
31. d	32. b	33. d	34. d	35. a	36. b				

Chapter 5

1. b	2. d	3. c	4. a	5. d	6. d	7. d	8. d	9. b	10. b
11. a	12. d	13. d	14. c	15. d	16. d	17. b	18. d	19. b	20. d
21. c	22. d	23. d	24. c	25. c	26. a	27. a	28. d	29. d	30. d
31. a	32. d								

Chapter 6

1. b	2. a	3. b	4. d	5. c	6. d	7. a	8. a	9. d	10. d
11. b	12. d	13. d	14. c	15. d	16. d	17. d	18. d	19. d	20. d
21. a	22. c	23. a	24. d	25. d	26. d	27. d	28. d	29. b	30. a
31. d	32. a	33. c							

Chapter 7

1. a	2. d	3. d	4. d	5. b	6. d	7. a	8. a	9. c	10. d
11. d	12. b	13. d	14. b	15. b	16. d	17. d	18. d	19. a	20. c
21. b	22. b	23. a	24. d	25. d	26. d	27. d	28. a	29. d	30. d
31. c	32. a	33. c	34. b	35. d	36. d	37. d	38. c	39. a	40. b
41. b	42. d	43. c	44. a	45. b	46. b				

ANSWER KEY

Chapter 8

1. d	2. c	3. c	4. d	5. b	6. d	7. a	8. b	9. b	10. d
11. b	12. d	13. d	14. d	15. b	16. a	17. b	18. d	19. b	20. d
21. d	22. b	23. d	24. b	25. d	26. d	27. a	28. d	29. a	30. d
31. d	32. a	33. d	34. b	35. d	36. c	37. d	38. c	39. a	40. d
41. d	42. d	43. d	44. d	45. d	46. d	47. d	48. c	49. a	50. c
51. b	52. d	53. b	54. b	55. c	56. c	57. d	58. b	59. d	

Chapter 9

1. a	2. d	3. b	4. d	5. d	6. c	7. b	8. c	9. a	10. d

Chapter 10

1. d	2. b	3. a	4. d	5. d	6. b	7. c	8. b	9. d	10. d
11. d	12. d	13. c	14. d	15. a	16. a	17. d			

Chapter 11

1. d	2. b	3. b	4. d	5. b	6. d	7. c	8. d	9. a	10. d
11. c	12. d	13. d	14. c	15. d	16. d	17. d	18. d	19. b	20. d
21. d	22. b	23. d	24. d	25. d	26. c	27. c	28. b	29. a	30. c
31. d	32. d	33. b	34. a	35. b	36. b	37. d	38. a	39. d	40. b
41. d	42. b	43. a	44. b	45. d	46. a	47. b	48. d	49. d	50. c
51. d	52. d	53. d	54. c	55. d	56. d	57. d	58. c	59. d	60. d
61. d	62. d	63. d	64. d	65. b	66. d	67. a	68. d	69. c	70. b
71. c	72. d	73. d	74. d						

www.ingramcontent.com/pod-product-compliance
Lightning Source LLC
Chambersburg PA
CBHW082043230426
43670CB00016B/2756